Military Politics
In Nigeria

MILITARY POLITICS IN NIGERIA

Economic Development and Political Stability

Theophilus Olatunde Odetola

Transaction Books
New Brunswick, New Jersey

Copyright © 1978 by Transaction, Inc.
New Brunswick, New Jersey 08903

Library of Congress Catalog Number: 76-58232
ISBN: 0-87855-100-X (cloth)
Printed in the United States of America

Library of Congress Cataloging in Publication Data

Odetola, Theophilus Olatunde.
    Military Politics in Nigeria.

    A revision of the author's thesis, Rutgers University
1967.
    Includes bibliographical references and index.
    1.   Nigeria—Politics and government—1960.
2.   Nigeria—Economic conditions.   3.   Nigeria—
Armed Forces—Political activity.   I.   Title.
JQ3083.1978.033   1978   320.9'669'05   76-58232
ISBN 0-87855-100-X

Contents

List of Illustrations

Acknowledgments

This book is a revised form of my doctoral dissertation written at Rutgers University in 1973.

It is difficult to decide who to thank among the many people who have helped in the preparation and writing of this book, and probably more difficult to know in what order to thank them. The list of people ranges from my children, whose occasional disturbances helped to take my mind off the work from time to time, to Professor Irving Louis Horowitz, whose tremendous courage and prodding have seen me through this work.

My sincere appreciation goes to the following: Irving Louis Horowitz, not only for his advice and great interest in my work, but also for the opportunity to learn the fortitude and courage which research in social science often requires. I have come to regard him not only as a great scholar but also as a friend. My thanks go to Harry Bredemeier, whose incisive and critical, scholarly approach to academic work I have come to respect and admire. I am also grateful to Ross Baker, Barbara Callaway, and Barbara Lewis, who have offered suggestions at various levels.

I also thank Dr. Jones Akinpelu, Messrs. Ilemobayo Akinnola, J. A. Omigbodun, and J. A. Afolabi, Mr. and Mrs. Egundeyi, Dr. and Mrs. Femi Ashley-Dejo, Dr. Ade Akintuyi, and Orobola Fasehun, who have helped in various capacities.

I am deeply grateful for the moral support I received from members of my family and in particular to Adebayo, Titilola, Adebanke, Omoladun, and my wife, Yetunde.

Introduction

During the 1960s, political stability broke down in many African states: economic development stagnated as a result of the flight of foreign capital. One response to the problem of instability was the military takeover, which occurred in a number of African nations (see Appendix 3). Many observers have questioned whether the military can be effective at establishing authority when the party system fails. In Nigeria, authority had broken down by December 1965, and the party system had lost the legitimacy to rule. General disarray in the polity resulted as open, premeditated, and violent murders of political opponents were carried out on the Nigerian streets. It became evident that the institutions of parliamentary government were unable to guarantee law and order. A system of government which has lost the capacity to guarantee minimal safety to many citizens cannot effectively coordinate and process the increasing demands that normally arise in a society, such as Nigeria, undergoing rapid social differentiation.

Since the civil war, public disturbances and riots in Nigeria have diminished. The simultaneous division of the nation into twelve states by the military has generated the need for coalitions cutting across ethnic boundaries. Many of the northern states lacked the administrative personnel possessed by some of the southern states, and an interstate exchange of personnel became one condition for establishing new relationships. The creation of states also helped to direct the demands for ethnic minority rights into organizational channels and laid the bases for communal integration. Moreover, the average annual growth rate since 1970 has been 8 percent per annum — twice that of any prewar year.[1]

What is it about the military that enables it to fulfill the role of rulers, however temporarily? Can the mere physical presence of the military account for the political quiescence, stability, and economic development that have so far been achieved in Nigeria? As we shall demonstrate in the following pages, the military has achieved coordination and effectiveness and established authority and legitimacy, not by simple physical threats but primarily by adapting its organizational characteristics to command a different type of collectivity. While the military has retained its traditional organizational characteristics of order, discipline, and hierarchy, it is responding to organizational requirements of compromise and persuasion, due in part to internal structural changes and in part to the influence of the civilian polity which it is now ruling.

Besides systematically regulating political demands in a rapidly changing environment, the military has generated accountability, and has streamlined and centralized decision making. This kind of coercion is a prerequisite of rule and is not always coterminous with dictatorship.[2]

Western analysts have tended to postulate a government and a "loyal opposition" along parliamentary lines as a basis for legitimate rule. The use of coercion as an instrument of rule has consequently been neglected and an undue emphasis has been placed on "consensus." Development literature only recently appears to have recognized this deficiency in the analysis of third-world development.[3]

In analyses of the economic and political development of newly independent African nations, theory has lagged behind reality. When many African nations became independent of colonial rule in the early 1960s, political analysts constructed models and typologies for African development. First, they postulated a multiparty system with a government and a loyal opposition. This party system soon exhibited signs of failure because it reflected the pluralism and distrust characteristic of the national scene. Political competition ensued. Next, because of the observable demand for rapid political and economic development, these theorists recognized the need for mobilization and developed typologies which immediately became distinguishable by the variable of "dynamism." We began to hear of "revolutionary centralizing systems,"[4] "revolutionary mass regime movement,"[5] "mobilization systems,"[6] and so on, all defined in terms of the characteristics of the party system.

Due to their preoccupation with the party system, the creators of these typologies conceived of revolutionary and mobilizing systems as the instrument by which legitimacy could be achieved, by creating a sense of commitment and by pervading the lives of the people or getting down to the grass roots through organizing a hierarchical, one-party system. But it became clearer that even though the one-party system is authoritarian, its domain is demonstrably limited.[7] On the whole, the one-party regime possesses little authority. The one-party system does not encompass the entire political system in which it operates. Many times it does not even get things done. At the local levels, civilian-led one-party systems showed early signs of weakness. The party organs were unable to generate a desirable level of national commitment, and very often directives emanating from the central party organs were ignored at the local levels.

In Nigeria, the military has approached highly controversial issues such as the allocation of resources and the national census less with a show of force than with a spirit of readiness to handle divisive issues. As we shall demonstrate in this study, the military is building institutions which are the foundations of political stability and economic development, rather than merely achieving a kind of "managed consensus" by fiat.

Ideology elements of nationalism, puritanism, and modernization are employed by the military as consciously expressive and symbolic gestures to generate a spirit of commitment to the idea of one nation in a society which had not yet achieved full integration. We will also emphasize differences in leadership styles between the military and former civilian leaders, by comparing charismatic legitimation and patrimonialism as explanatory tools for explaining the generation of authority and legitimacy in Nigeria.

ANALYTICAL FRAMEWORK

This study will focus on specific problem areas that are significant and sensitive with respect to political stability and economic development. Restricting our consideration to a limited range of topics will enhance the opportunity to analyze systematically, but fully, policy making and policy execution as practiced by the multiparty system and the military-bureaucratic system.

The areas selected, on account of their significance and sensitivity, are:

1.   National integration considered in terms of (1) communal or territorial integration (institution-building as integrative mechanism); (2) elite-mass integration, rural-urban integration; and (3) the building of political instruments and other political reforms. Divisions in the body politic of Nigeria occur along several lines: horizontally along ethnic lines (the civil war was fought largely along ethnic lines) and regional lines (there is a clear dichotomy between the city and the rural areas in terms of development); vertically across class strata, as reflected in the income distribution between the elite group and the masses of the people.

2.   The distribution of power between the federal government on the one hand and the state government on the other, together with the related problem of resource (finance, materials) allocation among the states. This relates to the problem of whether a strong center (with respect to constitutional authority) will more adequately solve the problem of political instability than a weak center, and thus it involves comparison of the present military-bureaucratic system (strong center and relatively

weaker states) with the prewar multiparty system (weak center and relatively stronger regions). The multiparty system collapsed in part because the regions were too strong. In the attempt to hold fast to their positions, the regions undermined the authority and the unity which the center represented. Similarly, the first military government collapsed because it made Nigeria a unitary state. Regions (states) were abolished and the provincial system (equivalent to the county governments in the United States) was created in their stead. We find, therefore, that two governments have fallen, in large part as a result of approaching the same problem from two different and extreme positions — one over-emphasizing the strength of the regions, the other of the center. The military-bureaucratic system has attempted to strengthen the center while yielding a measure of initiative and power to the newly created states. How has it allocated responsibilities, together with the means and sustenance to carry out such responsibilities? The specific topics that will be discussed then are: (1) patterns of power distribution between federal and states; (2) the politics of revenue allocation; and (3) the politics of the location of industries.

3.   Economic development: has the military-bureaucratic system come closer to achieving an economic breakthrough than the multiparty system? What is it about the military-bureaucratic system that may be responsible for a more rapid rise in per capita gross national product rate of investment, structural changes in industrialization, improvement in human resources as reflected in improvement in education, and the present position of agricultural development? Economic development is a primary goal of developing nations since it helps to demonstrate the government's capability and legitimacy to the masses of the people. We shall stress the structure of coercion as it enhances economic development: the directedness and pointedness with which the military moves into policy areas, and the strong accountability and supervision observable in the decision-making structure which is demanded both from military men and civilian officials. Such coercion also involves the regulation of demands which arise in a society undergoing rapid social, economic, and political differentiation. This regulation of demands at present rarely involves the use of physical force. In fact, there has been a dramatic decline in the use of such force in Nigeria since the end of the civil war between Nigerian federal forces and secessionist Biafra (comprising the present East Central, South East, and Rivers states). Emphasis has shifted to the use of persuasion and compromise in a complex political situation — a fact which reflects changes in a modernizing military structure, and also the military's ability to learn political bargaining while in the process of governing.

The attitude of the military toward foreign investment, on the one hand,

and economic nationalism, as dictated both by nationalist clamor for nationalization of foreign industries and the extent to which the military had attempted to reduce dependence on foreign sources of investment, on the other, will also be examined. Second, the military, as a source of power and authority, is always sensitive to pockets or groups which wield power in the society.[8] They are, therefore, concerned with the direction in which the economy is moving, in terms of which group appears to hold most economic power. It is a distinctive military style in politics to shift the economic development in a direction by which it could most easily be controlled by the state.

NATIONAL INTEGRATION

Problem of Communal Integration

The breakdown of public and political order in Nigeria between 1964 and 1966 led to a bitter civil war between secessionist Biafra and the rest of the federation of Nigeria. One of the crucial underlying issues was fear that one ethnic group would dominate another. Primordial ethnic loyalties took precedence over the idea of one Nigeria, and the political process was characterized by intense competition, corruption, and nepotism.

The ruling multiparty system reflected the schisms and divisions found in the body politic. Political parties (the National Council of Nigerian Citizens, the Action Group, and the Northern Peoples Congress) derived their authority from narrowly based ethnic groups and were in turn motivated to repay the loyalty of their clientele by means of political patronage. The political party in office at any one time not only represented a particular ethnic group, but distributed government offices to members of the ethnic group from which it derived its power. It became impossible to guarantee the rights of minority groups that had no political parties to represent their interests. There was, therefore, no single source of authority and this subsequent crisis of authority exacerbated the tensions.

What type of system generates sufficient authority to establish national integration? In Africa, the military is always a potential political factor since it can exert considerable force in the domestic vacuum; if it can be considered a national group, then it constitutes a reservoir of legitimate authority. In the Nigerian situation, it is difficult to see how anything short of some form of authoritarianism could maintain an integrated state.[9] Yet the military is not always capable of achieving order in developing nations. In Latin America, for example, the military may ally with oligarchic or middle-class groups to thwart change, and thus may be instrumental in generating political instability.[10]

The military government in Nigeria moved in 1967 to guarantee minority rights by destroying the old federal system of four regions (one of which was, by reason of population, more powerful than all the other regions combined) and creating twelve states in their place. The creation of states was consistently resisted by the political parties since it would reduce their effective areas of authority, but it was also a means of guaranteeing the rights of minority groups. Because it has no specific constituency to answer to, except the nation, the military has shown more concern for national needs than has the multiparty system, which has clung to little driblets of power.

An important source of political instability in Africa has been the lack of response to the political demands of ethnic minorities.[11] These demands substantively consist of the need for recognition of their political and economic rights as reflected in the equitable sharing of governmental resources. The creation of states has helped to channel and articulate these demands and has reduced political tension.

The military is traditionally a bureaucratic institution which often attempts to govern the civilian polity by bureaucratic coordination. Bureaucratic coordination may be an effective mode of operation in situations where political, economic, and social differentiation are rapidly taking place.[12] One consequence of such a mode of operation is that the Nigerian military government has established national commissions in several subject areas (such as education, agriculture, finance, personnel, and establishment) to act as forums wherein different states could air their differences, as well as explore common interests. The balanced composition of these commissions is reflected in the military, civilian, political-ethnic, and academic backgrounds of their members. Each commission meets several times a year and makes recommendations with far-reaching policy implications. As a result of these meetings, communication has been improved at the intergovernmental and ethnic levels. In the multiparty system, the effort by the political parties (all ethnically based) to secure their respective areas of authority against "outside" influences was reflected in respective trade and personnel exchange laws.

Another consequence of the bureaucratic mode of operation is the strengthening, enlargement, and differentiation of the several existing bureaucratic institutions of government. As we shall demonstrate in the following chapters, the military government has made more break-throughs in protecting minority interests than did the multiparty system before it. The Nigerian federal government is building political and bureaucratic instruments that enhance communication among the various ethnic groups and strengthen bureaucratic institutions.

The problem of the gap between the small elite group of professionals, intellectuals, businessmen, and bureaucrats, on the one hand, and the masses of peasants, small artisans, and so on will be approached at two levels: (1) the income differential and the real disparity in living styles observable between the two groups; and (2) the rural-urban dichotomy characterized by migration to the cities, and the increasing problem of employment.

Elite-Mass Income Differential. A significant structural imbalance in the economy and the polity is the great differential in income distribution between the higher and lower income groups. Since the majority of the Nigerian peoples receive a low income (less than $300 per annum), the small group receiving a high income stand in bold relief to the rest of the society. Their conspicuous life-style highlights the differential access to power between the two groups. Because of their poorer access to employment, many new immigrants to the cities remain jobless and join the ever-expanding urban proletariat. The urban proletariat is easily manipulated by any interest group that might want to use it to foment political violence. In this way, it is a potential source of political instability.

The higher-paid category (earning $2,500 and over) is less than 0.5 percent of the total population. About 75 percent of Nigerians are engaged in subsistence agriculture; per capita income in agriculture has been shown to be the lowest. Income from commerce is the highest. Between 1960 and 1967, the average income in manufacturing and construction grew to almost three times as much as that in agriculture, and the average income in commerce grew to as much as seven times that of agriculture. The wage differential between skilled and unskilled categories has also tended to widen. The ratio was 1.7:1 in 1962, but by 1967 it had risen to 2:1. Permanent secretaries and university professors earn almost thirty times as much as unskilled workers.[13] The differentials that now exist are not justifiable on an economic or an equity basis.[14]

Is the military motivated to reduce this income gap or to act in favor of the elite group to which it is a party? The theoretical argument in support of a military that is attuned to populist demands is based, in part, on the changing pattern of recruitment into the armed forces. Horowitz, Johnson, and Halpern have argued that in the emerging nations of Africa, Asia, and Latin America, the military tends to recruit from dispossessed groups and from elements demanding rapid social mobility. This would tend to make it less elitist than, for instance, the British military.[15]

While, in general, the recruitment pattern may have changed and the military may now be less elitist, the empirical link between social origin and subsequent political behavior is not easy to demonstrate. Nordlinger has argued that experiences of deprivation and marginality instill impetus for individual mobility rather than a broader concern with the plight of the less fortunate.[16] Horowitz presented only the empirical facts and did not make the conceptual jump between social background and subsequent political behavior,[17] but it is theoretically important to explain why some militaries support the new or traditional classes and others support the masses. We propose to invoke the theoretical link between the military's motivation to seize power and its subsequent military performance. Bienen has argued that one determinant of the military group's capacity for governing is the motivation which led that group to stage a coup in the first place. If the military, or one element of it, makes a coup because it has a specific program for modernizing society that it feels it can carry out, then it is possible to more fully understand its performance as a governing group.[18] An ostensible reason why the Nigerian military seized power was because the political elite was corrupt and had amassed wealth "at the expense" of the masses.[19] It can thus be assumed that the military had some definite program for carrying out a reduction of the elite-mass income differential. An analysis of the internal dynamics of coups is a useful guide to the military's subsequent political action.

Rural-Urban Dichotomy and Problem of Unemployment. The development in many emerging nations has encouraged the growth of urban centers as the foci of industrial activity, relative to the rural areas. One concomitant development is growing urban unemployment. Unemployment has been characterized by the migration of young people to the cities in search of wage-earning jobs. This has resulted in an increased crime rate, overcrowding, and pressure on the public utilities. The urban population has been observed to be growing at two to four times the national rate. Slightly more than 80 percent of the unemployed were in the cities in 1969-1970. In the same year, while 8 percent of the estimated labor force was unemployed, less than 0.5 percent of the rural labor force was unemployed.[20]

The twin problems of (1) a great differential in income distribution between the elite and the masses, and (2) the rural-urban differential, may be resolved by a number of approaches:

1. Revise the national income structure in such a way as to reduce the observable gap. Since both the multiparty system and the military regime have revised the income structure on an ad hoc basis, we will compare their policy guidelines for such revisions to infer the likely bearing of the different guidelines on the elite-mass income gap and the rural-urban gap.

2. Generate increased employment through industry and the

dispersion of industrial projects into the rural areas. As we shall see, the Nigerian military government has generated a capacity for industrial growth proportionately higher than the multiparty system did in a comparative period of time.

3. Improve agriculture. This seems to be the key to the development of rural areas. Some Middle Eastern and Latin American military regimes have undertaken land reform programs to improve the condition of the peasants and hold down migration to the cities. Agricultural development seems to have stagnated in Nigeria since the end of the civil war for a number of reasons. The military government, however, is attempting to arrest this decline by major policy decisions, such as the setting up of agricultural credit banks.

The net effect of these policies should be the reduction of industrial strikes, peasant revolts, protest demonstrations, and other evidence of political unrest. One must argue that the military government's ban on strikes has been instrumental in producing this effect, but strikes and lockouts still occur in great numbers and the ban has been highly ineffective. The reduction in the number of strikes is not simply a consequence of direct military physical threat. Industrial unrest, mob violence, and political assassinations have in fact been reduced substantially over the number that took place during the multiparty regime, due to the more effective policy decisions taken by the military government to correct the imbalance of income differentials and rural-urban development differentials. The policy decisions of the military governments have been more effective because they have been directed at the root of the problem. For example, farmers have frequently rioted because of the system by which they are paid for their export products. The marketing board, an intermediary body between the farmer and the foreign buyer, was used by the party system as a reservoir from which money could be used, not only for party purposes but also to subsidize other sectors of the economy. The farmer was thus bearing the burden of the economy in tax subsidies to relatively richer sectors. The federal military government removed this function of the marketing board and made payments directly to the farmer. The result has been a rise in income to farmers and a reduction in farmer-originated riots and disturbances. Other examples will be given in chapters substantively dealing with this problem.

DISTRIBUTION OF POWER AND RESOURCE ALLOCATION

Patterns of Power Distribution and Political Stability

With the creation of many new states, new problems arose in Nigeria.

How would activities be coordinated? Should there be a strong or weak federal center? What were the implications of power distribution for the exercise of authority in a divided pluralist society? What political changes had been brought about by the new system and what new social processes had been set in motion?

While the military government was faced with the problem of establishing order and effective authority, it also had to ensure the close participation of the state governments. Before the civil war, the party system ensured that the regions were more powerful than the center — a situation that tended to exacerbate regional and ethnic differences. Each regional government attempted to encroach upon the power of the federal center by inching into areas that were the concern of the center. This led to unnecessary duplication, unhealthy competition, and so on in such areas as higher education, interregional trade, hiring of personnel, and attraction of foreign investment. The authority of the federal government was undermined.

The military values of order, centralized policy making, and decentralized initiatives are uniquely suited to the needs of integration and coordination, as well as the achievement of effectiveness.[21] As in Burma, Pakistan, and Brazil, the military moved in to coordinate activities by taking control of areas that had significant and broad national policy implications. At the same time, it was aware of the need to let each state function properly in those areas considered to be of purely local interest and to let each state share in policy making at the national level. In its efforts to achieve coordination and effectiveness, the federal military government has moved to take control of policy matters considered to be of wide national interest. At the same time, state governments retain control over local matters. Thus, centralization has proceeded simultaneously with decentralization of functions and roles.

The basic problem is how to differentiate areas of responsibility. In the old multiparty system, each region had areas of responsibility constitutionally allocated to it. Such areas of activity were termed "residual" and included such subjects as trade and agriculture. Areas that were administered by the federal government were termed "exclusive" and included responsibility for the determination of foreign policy. The twilight zone over which both the regional and federal government had joint jurisdiction (pre-1967) was termed "concurrent." In the concurrent list were such matters as higher education and the attraction of foreign investments. The competitive nature of the political process before the civil war led to the granting of highly competitive trading and mining concessions to overseas investors, and to the duplication of university programs in the face of scarce resources and nationally low recruitment possibilities. The different states recognized the need for coordinated policy making for higher education and foreign investment: the poorer states because they could no longer afford to lag behind; the richer states because they appreciated that increased uneven development could only lead to further instability. This is not to argue that they acquiesced to stagnation, but they did accept the limited opportunity allowed for competition as reflected in federal government policies concerning foreign investment.

Politics of Resource Allocation and Structure of Power Distribution

The successful administration of the areas of responsibility noted above is contingent upon the amount of revenue each state receives. This, in turn, depends upon the amount derived from the general national revenue. This dependency, coupled with the unhealthy competitive character of group relationships at the ethnic level, generated an atmosphere of intense sensitivity, mutual distrust, and even hostility, during the civilian government era.

The sharing of revenue is a central reason for Nigeria's instability. Between 1946 and 1964, no less than three fiscal commissions were set, each revising the work of its predecessor and each working out new formulas for the distribution of resources. Significantly, as new resources (for instance, oil) were discovered, the party, and therefore the region that benefited most put intense pressure on the national government to revise the formula so that the region would receive the lion's share of benefits from the resources in its territory. Extreme regional self-interest and obscurantism dominated public issues and political decisions, and this was one of the immediate causes of the civil war. Since there was no sense of national purpose, regional and local needs took precedence over matters of national interest.

In Nigeria, the government has not only devised an ad hoc formula which deals with specific local products. It has also given the center more money to cope with increasing areas of responsibility and more money to give to the states than the states ever received in the multiparty days. The aim, however, is to give the federal government greater leverage in making uniform policies in specific areas such as higher education and foreign investment.

The federal government is becoming financially stronger than the states.[22] It has streamlined overlapping productions: in the economic field it has discouraged the duplication of identical industrial projects — a situation that was prevalent during multiparty regimes; due to ethnic

XXI

rivalry, it has improved the tax structure (as will be elaborated in Chapter 6); and it has increased revenue from oil. Thus the Nigerian federal military government has far more financial strength in comparison to the states than the multiparty system had in comparison to the regions.

ECONOMIC DEVELOPMENT AND RELATED PROBLEMS

Economic Breakthrough: Military versus Multiparty System

Economic development is widely recognized as a primary goal of the emerging nations of Africa, Asia, and Latin America. The multiparty system has proved incapable of achieving rapid economic breakthroughs in many of these nations. In a recent comparative analysis, Horowitz showed that coercive authority correlated well with high development, while democratic rule correlated well with low development.[23] He argued that, in the examples cited, the amount of explained variance that the military factor yields is much higher than the classical literature would allow for; he concluded that the political structure of coercion seems to be a more decisive factor in explaining the gross national product than any factor of production in any third world system per se. The element of coercion is directly linked to the character of military domination. Since the military took over power in Nigeria and Brazil, the gross national product has risen by more than 100 percent in each case.

Horowitz has argued that the military demands a highly efficient economy yet insists on remaining the touchstone for determining the nature of the economy.[24] What specific mechanisms does it employ to achieve an efficient economy? As argued earlier, the military often operates by means of the bureaucratic model. In Nigeria, it has altered the structure of economic decision making (as will be elaborated later) so as to exercise direct supervision over channels of reporting and accountability. It has also coordinated and streamlined all the activities of economic agencies in such a way that weaknesses in the economy are detected more easily than during the multiparty regime.

When weaknesses are detected or new orientations are planned, the military moves into direct, nonequivocating action by initiating and executing policies to remedy or advance such areas. A recent example is the current state of the agricultural sector. The military government appreciated the enormity of the situation and, after seeking advice from experts from the United Nations and local officials, moved in with specific policies, such as the establishment of an Agricultural Development Credit Bank to grant loans to farmers. In the industrial sector, the military government created special agencies that are directly accountable to it with respect to the expansion of industrial infrastructure, such as road construction. Thus, there are two ways in which this mechanism works. First, the process of direct supervision and accountability to the military government induces an aura of an efficient, rigorous method of operation in the agencies. Second, the military characteristic of direct intervention, by means of initiating policy, executing it, and following it up, has produced dramatic results. Such results as the rise in gross national product have had the consequence of assuring people of the capability of the military.

Character of Economic Development: Military versus Multiparty System

There appears to be little controversy about the role of the military in developing heavy industry, as opposed to consumer industry. Many writers have argued that the military is not only interested in building up its own hardwares but performs special roles in nation building, such as initiating highway construction, national communication networks, and other heavy engineering projects. The movement towards large-scale industrializations uniquely links the military and the economy. Horowitz asserts that "the military is that sector which dampens consumerism . . . and promotes instead forms of developmentalism that moves towards such consumer items as automobiles and television sets."[25] Such trends could be observed in Nasser's Egypt, Ataturk's Turkey, Ayub Khan's Pakistan, as well as in Burma and Brazil (as evidenced by the construction of dams and irrigation projects in those nations). The significance of the development of heavy industry is that it lays the framework and infrastructure for further development rather than for investment in consumable goods. However, in most third world countries, the civilian politician appears to have been desirous of establishing consumer-type industrial projects (for instance, Nigeria was the first country in Africa, including South Africa, to establish a television station) in order to attract the direct support of their constituents. In other words, many developing countries appear to be enjoying the consumable items of the advanced nations although they have not gone through the process of laying the foundation and infrastructure for such development.

Economic Nationalism and Foreign Investment

Capital for investment is scarce in many African countries, yet the rhetoric and oftentimes the reality of development is highly nationalistic (for instance, in the ultimate nationalization of many foreign enterprises). How does any government reconcile the need to attract foreign investment with the desire to satisfy nationalist aspirations? Most governments must either yield to nationalist pressure by nationalizing foreign enterprises and losing future investment possibilities, or face charges of being labelled antinationalist, neocolonial, imperialist agents. Such charges are made on the grounds that the dependence generated does not really generate local capital but that it drains away the little capital that was available to the foreign investor's country.

While its long-term objective seems to be nationalist control of the economy, the Nigerian military is moving only cautiously in that direction. The military government still actively encourages foreign investment, but it also fosters economic independence through a number of deliberate policy decisions. The 1970-1974 development plan emphasizes controlling the "heights of the Nigerian economy"[26] by demanding to own a minimum of 35 percent of equity shares in all existing industries and the controlling shares in all new foreign enterprises. At the same time that it is moving in the direction of increasing economic independence, the military government has not nationalized foreign enterprises. This is the policy emphasized in the public statements of such men as Dr. Nnamdi Azikiwe, the former president of the nation; Chief Obafemi Awolowo, the former commissioner for finance; and the deputy governor of the Central Bank, who declared that "Nigeria would prefer increased participation in foreign industries than outright nationalization."[27] Such statements are reassuring to foreign investors who do not perceive the investment climate as immediately threatening and are ready to go along with more indigenous control.

In the years immediately before the civil war, foreign investment trickled to a minimum because of the perceived political instability. The inordinate dependence on foreign sources of investment resulted in a severely threatened economy with the withdrawal of foreign investment.

The Nigerian military government's move toward greater economic independence can succeed if sufficient local capital can be generated. The military government has developed policies that generate more internal capital resources than did the multiparty system by overhauling the internal revenue collection system; increasing the tax paid by companies and corporations; initiating policy whereby foreign companies would have to reinvest a substantial portion of the profits into local projects; and encouraging local banks by giving them favorable investment considerations in the face of strong competition from more powerful foreign banks. In the times before the civil war, many local banks folded because they could not compete with foreign banks. This new policy has stimulated local investment. A policy which has generated internal capital is that of plowing back substantial portions of oil revenue into local industrial development. The government annually receives considerable foreign exchange from oil revenues, sufficient by itself to discourage dependence on foreign sources of capital.

The result is that the military government, in implementing its first four-year development plan, has been able to place emphasis on local and internal resources. It has been able to plan and has derived more than 60 percent of the revenue for implementation from local resources, in contrast to less than 20 percent achieved in either of the two development plans launched by the multiparty system prior to 1966.[28]

Public versus Private Economy

In general, economic development in Nigeria has always taken the form of a mixture of private and public enterprise. Theoretically, the unique linkage between the military and the economy often induces the military to favor public over private economy (for example, the military needs industrial technology for its own use). Encouraging the private sector over the public would generate a competitive class or induce undue dependence on private citizenry. Since the military controls the state and the producers (private or public) have a special relation to the state, by going public the military limits the ability of private industry to perform a countervailing role.[29]

Policy decisions, such as injecting more money into public enterprise relative to that obtained before the civil war, and setting up public corporations in those areas where private investment does not appear to be doing well, indicate that the government seems to be encouraging greater interest in public as opposed to private enterprise. Individuals in the decision-making cadre have made numerous statements against private enterprise. The federal trade commissioner made the following comment: "The supposed beauty of private enterprise and the passive role of the state in economic life is a snare and a myth. Untramelled private enterprise can be a bane, wreaking fearful havoc on the vast majority of the people."[30]

The military government has no intention of discouraging private enterprise when it shows signs of making a headway. The Nigerian Industrial Development Bank, for example, was set up to grant loans to private businessmen. The idea seems to be that the government at this stage is more capable of supporting new enterprises (especially in equity share contributions to foreign-owned enterprises) than are indigenous private investors. The overall trend seems to be in the direction of a more socialist, state-owned economy.

NOTES

1. *Africa Research Bulletin,* February 1973.
2. Apter, David, *Choice and the Politics of Allocation* (New Haven, 1971).

3. Horowitz, Irving Louis, *Three Worlds of Development* (New York: Oxford University Press, 1972), ch. 12. Also Apter, David, *The Politics of Modernization . . . Choice and the Politics of Allocation* (New Haven, 1971).

4. Coleman, James and Rosberg, Carl, *Political Parties and National Integration in Tropical Africa* (Berkeley and Los Angeles, 1966), pp. 1-12.

5. Tucker, R. C., "On Revolutionary Movement Regimes," in his *Soviet Political Mind* (New York, 1963), pp. 3-19.

6. Apter, David, *The Political Kingdom of Uganda* (Princeton, N. J.: Princeton University Press, 1961), pp. 21-24.

7. Zolberg, Aristide, *Creating Political Order: The Party States of West Africa* (Chicago, 1966).

8. Horowitz, *Three Worlds.*

9. No source of authority retained any form of legitimacy by January 1966.

10. Lieuwen, E., *Arms and Politics in Latin America* (New York, 1960). Nun, N., "The Middle Class Military Coup," in C. Veliz, ed., *the Politics of Conformity* (New York, 1967), pp. 323-56.

11. Congo and Ghana are examples.

12. Weber, Max, *The Theory of Social and Economic Organizations* (New York, 1957), p. 363. Bredemeier, Harry C., *Personality and Social Systems*, in press. Blau, P., and Scott, C., *Formal Organizations* (San Francisco, 1962).

13. *West Africa*, April 14, 1973.

14. These differentials were inherited from the colonial days and perpetuated by the present systems.

15. Horowitz, *Three Worlds*, ch. 12. Johnson, J. J., *Continuity and Change in Latin America* (Stanford, 1964). Halpern, M., "Middle Eastern Armies and the New Middle Class," in J. J. Johnson, *The Role of the Military in Underdeveloped Nations* (Princeton, 1962).

16. Nordlinger, Eric, "Soldiers in Mufti: The Impact of Military Rule Upon Economic and Social Change in Non-Western States," *American Political Science Review 64* (1970): 1131-48.

17. Horowitz, *Three Worlds*, ch. 12.

18. Bienen, Henry, ed., *The Military and Modernization* (Chicago: Atherton 1971), pp. x-xxv.

19. Major Nzeogwu, *New Nigeria* (Kaduna 17, January, 1966).

20. Teriba, O. and Phillips, D. A., "Income Distribution and National Integration in Nigeria," *Nigerian Journal of Economic and Social Studies*, 13 (1971): pp. 77-122.

21. Horowitz, *Three Worlds*, ch. 12.

22. This has enabled it to make far-reaching decisions affecting the whole federation.

23. Horowitz, *Three Worlds*, ch. 12.

24. Ibid.

25. Ibid.

26. Second National Development Plan, Lagos, 1970.

27. Asabia, A., *Central Bank of Nigeria Quarterly Report*, March 1972.

28. First report of the 1970-1974 Nigeria National Development Plans, Lagos, June 1972.

29. Horowitz, *Three Worlds*, ch. 12.

30. Shagari, Shehu, *West Africa*, April 14, 1972.

Military Politics In Nigeria

Chapter 1
Military Politics in
the Third World

Political sociology concerning the role of the military in developing nations is still in its infancy. The paucity of useful theory derives from the following factors: (1) the lack of clarity in defining concepts such as political development; (2) the conservative bias of political analysts, by which any deviation from democratic norms, or the introduction of elements of coercion in the process of government, is considered abnormal; and (3) the lack of intensive study of the internal dynamics of military coups which would shed light on the motives of coup leaders and on their ability to learn the art of political bargaining, once in power. If many African, Asian, and Latin American countries are suffering from crises of authority, can the military succeed in establishing authority? If so, what are the implications for a democratic theory of social development?

The Nigerian military-bureaucratic regime has advanced political development by fostering national integration and by building political institutions. This notion is antithetical to the established ideas of political scientists who hold that the military is incapable of such development.[1]

The turbulence produced by rapid modernization and the problem of governing in a modernizing society require a system that contains elements of coercion if government is to be effective and show authority, even if such coercion is sometimes accompanied by persuasion and compromise.[2] The issues raised by the notion of increased coercion create special problems for a democratic theory of society, insofar as it applies to developing nations.

An analysis of the dynamics of a military coup (that is, such elements as motivation to rule, degree of factionalism, and so on) is important for theory assessing subsequent military performance.[3] The confused state of theory about military performance has resulted, in part, from the fact that some analysts did not consider the military as an interest group capable of seizing power for corporate interests, while others did appreciate that the military served as a nationalist group motivated by the need to develop the nation. The military can learn political bargaining and can, as an organization, be influenced by the political processes of the society which it is governing. Hence, it can be a governing body and not simply a caretaker group.

THE MILITARY AND POLITICAL DEVELOPMENT

Most political sociologists appear to be negative about the ability of military rulers to build political institutions which would foster political development. One school of thought holds that the military is often hostile or indifferent to fostering political development by building political institutions. Prominent in this school is Huntington, who asserts that military officers are "frequently indifferent or hostile to the needs of political institution building . . . they are ill-prepared to make fundamental changes in political processes and institutions."[4] Other scholars argue that the military is incapable or inept. Nordlinger says that the military views politics as regulated conflict, "in which competition and compromise is transformed into the apolitical politics of concensus, acquiescence and government by fiat."[5] Feld argues that the goal of political stability sought by the military "is the stability of a vacuum, a state undisturbed by the erratic movement of partisan bodies."[6]

In the last fifteen years, political sociologists have focused upon the emerging, developing nations of the third world in the effort to explicate the meaning of political development. They focus specifically upon an analysis of those political and economic processes in the postcolonial development of the third world nations. Political development is conceived of, therefore, as deriving from the framework of modernization — a broad and widely misused concept that embraces political, social, and economic changes in these societies.

According to these analysts, modernization consists of such changes as urbanization, literacy, and industrial changes. These aspects of modernization (conceived of as processes) are, in turn, considered basic factors in the generation of increased political participation and mobilization of the masses in the new urban centers. Emphasis has been placed on modernization and the associated concept of mobilization and increased participation. For example, Deutsch argues that modernization involves social mobilization and "this complex process of social changes in significantly correlated with major changes in politics . . . modernization means mass mobilization, mass mobilization means increased political participation and increased political participation is the key element of political development."[7] Rustow argues that political development can be defined as an increasing political unity plus a broadening base of participation.[8] Riggs defines political development as the process of politicization, that is, the "increasing participation or involvement of the citizen in state activities."[9] Almond and Verba argue that in all new nations of the world, the belief that ordinary men ought to be involved participants in the political system is widespread, and they conceive of political development as the participation of large groups of people who have previously been outside of politics in the political system.[10]

The implicit assumption in the above formulations is that the relationship between economic modernization (improved manpower through literacy, urbanization, an improved communication network, and so on.) and political development is positive, since these improvements will lead to mobilization and participation. Economic modernization increases political development.

This formulation has weaknesses. It does not account for changes that may occur in societies where economic modernization may not be taking place at an intensity that leads to urbanization, observable industrial changes, and so on (as in many slowly evolving traditional societies). In societies like the United States where rapid modernization is relatively absent, there should be little or no political development. Secondly, mobilization and increased political participation have been known to precipitate unstable political conditions, phenomena that are not conducive to political development.

An increased rate of economic development often leads to political instability, since it tends to induce a rising level of demands from organized groups like trade unions, student and peasant movements, urban proletariats, and ethnic groups, which demand better pay, expansion of educational opportunities, governmental investment in local projects, and a general rise in standards of living.[11] Improved communication, which follows economic development, raises the expectations and organizational ability of such groups.[12]

The destabilizing effects of economic development operate at various levels. First, certain preexisting conflicts have been exacerbated, especially by the politics of competition which has followed upon economic development in many African nations. Questions about the equitability of aid from the center to the regions, or about whether certain states are more entitled to favorable treatment than others because they are more backward, take on increasingly poignant political overtones.

Second, some preexisting relationships are altered or changed completely. In developing nations, economic development has substantially raised industrial output at a rate faster than production of food, cost of living in the cities, and the rate of migration to the cities and subsequent unemployment. The problem of migration into the cities has been compounded by rising inflation, both of which have led to strikes, demonstrations, and violence.

The expansion of educational facilities as a result of economic development increases recruitment into the educated elite cadre. As Hoselitz and Weiner have pointed out with respect to India, this situation tends to widen the impact of mass media, opening up new communication networks which then may establish new contacts and form the bases of new groups or reinforce old ones. "In other words, economic development produces as a by product . . . the leadership of groups and the organizational independence from British rule, the improving economic conditions have not narrowed the existing gaps but widened them and increased the political instability that derived from them."[13] A government can respond by attempting to satisfy these demands and pursuing a developmental policy, but no government (especially in developing areas) possesses enough resources to satisfy all demands. A development-centered policy, per se, cannot lead to any significant lessening of political instability. Even though governmental resources may increase, demands (almost always expressed in political terms) tend to increase simultaneously, sometimes more rapidly than resources. As shown above, organizations making demands are likely to proliferate and increase in size and power. As Hoselitz and Weiner[14] have argued, decisive steps that will show results reside in the ability of government to regulate demands by political action. Horowitz and Apter have both argued that comparative development theory suggests that rapid modernization requires increased coercion.[15] This theoretical point will increasingly unfold and be elaborated as we try to explicate the meaning of political development.

Rejecting the concepts of mobilization and participation as the principal ingredients of political development, Huntington has suggested that political development consists essentially in structural differentiation and institutionalization of the processes of government.[16] Yet no case study (of which we are aware) has examined the theoretical basis of his assertion. This study has attempted to fill that vacuum and thus to advance the state of theory by clarifying conceptual confusions that have stood in the way of further progress. Paradoxically, we have employed some of Huntington's conceptualization to disprove his assertion about military performance.

The focus on procedures and roles which develop or merge from the effort of a political system to tackle or adapt to more complex tasks and functions clearly point to development, since it emphasizes the increased capacity of the system to deal with new situations. Political development, as used here, is closely related to the capacity of emerging nations at any time in their history to deal with the problems which increased modernization may generate. As structural differentiation occurs in the political system, the need for increased coordination, accountability, authority, and legitimizing such authority increases. The generation of increased capacity to deal with new political situations can be seen to lie at the root of political development. Apter argues that the dynamic of modernization is that it is a process of increasing complexity in human affairs within which the polity must act.[17] Klinghoffer claims that political development is based on the ability of the state to cope with an increased modern environment—"the ability to act effectively in such a complex, modernized environment is political development."[18] Zolberg states that political development means the ability of government to create instruments that effectively reach the grass roots and help it to rule.[19]

Politics is a multifunctional phenomenon[20] and, as such, no single scale can be used to measure the degree of political development. It is necessary, therefore, to recall the two distinctive areas we have dealt with in this study: (1) the establishment of administrative institutions and the strengthening of the old; and (2) the building of political instruments to reach down to the grass roots.

MILITARY-BUREAUCRATIC SYSTEM VERSUS MULTIPARTY SYSTEM: EFFECTIVENESS, COERCION, AUTHORITY, AND LEGITIMACY

Is the Nigerian military-bureaucratic system governing effectively, or more effectively than the preceding multiparty system? The capacity of a government to perform is a measure of its effectiveness.[21]

Effectiveness can be measured in two analytical dimensions: (1) the mechanism by which a goal is reached; and (2) the outcomes of an action (that is, how significant or useful the outcomes are as products for the political system). We are employing the concept in both dimensions. As mechanism, its empirical referents would be such phenomena as the capacity of financial, material, political, and human resources; extractive capacity of tax, power resources, and so on; and decisiveness at crucial and opportune moments. As outcomes, the empirical referents of effectiveness are visible in such economic indices as changes in the amount of capital invested, the rate of growth of the gross national product, and so on.

Getting things done fast (that is, being effective) paradoxically generates increased political demands. We have used effectiveness here simply to mean efficient capability to produce and distribute certain outcomes (mainly economic). A theoretical problem arises: does governmental effectiveness guarantee political stability? The answer is, intriguingly, no. Governmental effectiveness in delivering goods to people may further political capacity, but it can also create new demand areas that become increasingly politicized. In fact, with an effective government, demands usually do become political in character. This is more true in a system where the government is the chief (if not the sole) source of supply of goods (economic resources, employment).[22] Almond and Powell argue that governmental effectiveness could lead to instability and a decline in political capacity, as was demonstrated in the relationship between economic development and political stability.[23]

If the pursuit of effectiveness as a means of leading to increased stability is not to be counterproductive, order must be maintained by means of systematic regulation of unanticipated, latent consequences, such as increased politicization of demands and resultant rioting. Demonstration effects and resultant demand for consumer goods are very great in emerging countries. Once these demands are politicized, the masses may be manipulated by both internal and external agents and forces. The argument is that the establishment of authority alongside the exhibition of efficiency become twin conditions for governing in third world environments, where not only ethnic and cultural pluralism but also the disruptive influences of rapid modernization create potentially unstable conditions. For any government to claim legitimacy, it must exhibit both effectiveness and authority. Authority will derive from the government's ability to institute systematic regulation of demands by a combination of coercion, persuasion, and manipulation. Once these forms of control are accepted, the ruled tend to suspend judgment when they are subsequently confronted with such controls (unless such controls become too harsh). Suspension of critical judgment when accepting commands or persuasion or advice reflects the acceptance of authority. A brief example will illustrate the points above.

The federal military government created twelve new states out of the four existing Nigerian regions to insure that no one ethnic group dominated others (as was the case in the multiparty system). Agitation developed for the creation of more states by ethnic groups or elite groups that stood to gain. The government responded by noting the demands, promising to investigate them, but emphatically refusing to do so until the present development plans, based upon the current state structure, were completed. They threatened any group that continued agitation (at least until after a specified period) with adequate reprisals. Thus, the government used a mixture of persuasion, manipulation, and coercion.

The crises of authority that have been observed in many African nations underline the shift from economic to political institutions that can legitimize decisions. Most economic programs are, today, direct consequences of political decisions. Military government has emerged as a direct consequence of the crises of authority and legitimacy, and they are holding the fort (however temporarily) better than a democratic party system based on a western model could have performed at this time. With the emergence of dedicated and competent (rather than obscurantist and inept) civilian leaders, the military may become less of a competitive alternative. For the present, military government is more suitable for third world countries, where rapid modernization and consumerism is occuring before the structural bases of development are consolidated.

In Nigeria, military authority and order are generally superimposed upon the political system. Policies are discussed in the federal cabinet (consisting of civilians and former politicans); policy statements are issued to state military governors who discuss them in state cabinets. These policies (often couched in decrees or edicts) are passed onto, processed, and interpreted by the civil service or special agencies. The policies are explained to the masses by the military governors, the bureaucracy, and the civil commissioners. This structure allows for processing of political demands, since civilian commissioners perform important liaison and brokerage functions.

Civilian commissioners consist of two categories: (1) old politicians who were proven clean by judicial tribunals set up by the military; and (2) young men who have had no previously known political affiliation. The discreditation of some older politicians and the co-optation of younger ones have presented symbolic ritual acts of purification which earned the government an initial basis of legitimacy.

The liaison function of the civilian commissioners is reinforced by the encouragement of an alert, if somewhat subdued public opinion. The head of state has asserted that he openly welcomes public debate on some selected issues and agrees not to initiate policy on such issues unless they are debated (although discussions on certain selected sensitive issues, such as the allocation of revenue, were not openly encouraged until a national census was completed and a constitutional conference invited).[24] To the credit of the military, movements that aggregate demands, such as peasant organizations, civil service unions, and trade unions have not only been allowed to exist but have even been encouraged. Some organizations which had previously been denied access to information by bureaucratic red tape found the military more responsive. This raises doubt about the assertion of many political analysts that only the party system is responsive to demands.

The atmosphere of persuasion that pervades the political climate in

Nigeria encourages public expression of demands. When such demands assume potentially disruptive dimensions, however, coercion is employed to regulate them. At what point does the regulation of demands become repression under a military regime? It is difficult to fix a point on the continuum from democratic practices on the one hand to authoritarianism on the other, but such indicators as the frequency and intensity of political agitations, demonstrations, and so on are sensitive measures to determine when people begin to feel repressed. Also, at such a point, the delicate balance between coercion and persuasion is disrupted and the governmental repressive apparatus (police arrests, imprisonment) becomes more active.

The need to establish authority is greatest on two specific occasions (in terms of judiciously regulating demands and fostering orderly progress): (1) in times of rapid modernization when the rate of change may cause instability; and (2) when a government shows efficiency and becomes effective, and demands consequently become increasingly political in complexion.

A demonstration of whether increasing effectiveness is matched by a corresponding degree of authority will help to show whether a regime is losing authority and how fast such loss may be taking place. Most previous analyses have insisted that the civilian regimes that failed in Africa—Nigeria, 1966; Ghana, 1966; Congo, 1964; Togo, 1964; and so on—did not possess authority *ab initio*.[25] Such an explanation is narrow since it fails to take account of the initial surge of enthusiasm and modernization which gave legitimacy to these regimes. That is, such regimes had legitimacy and, therefore, authority at the outset. Authority slipped from their grasp as they failed to cope with new political demands. The political process degenerated into unhealthy competition among various groups and finally collapsed. The multiparty system in Nigeria failed to develop new capabilities to handle increasing political demands; it resorted to highly repressive measures, crushing the opposition, jailing opposition leadership, and rigging elections. The party government was on the verge of passing a preventive detention act when public order broke down in the nation. This study shows that the present military-bureaucratic system responded quickly and effectively to political demands while developing the authority to regulate such demands.

DYNAMICS OF MILITARY COUPS, MILITARY CAPABILITY TO LEARN ON THE JOB, AND MILITARY PERFORMANCE

In general, theoretical debates over whether the military officers can modernize their societies have occurred in an empirical vacuum.

Theorizing has focused on two different but related themes: (1) explanation of military intervention; and (2) focus on the analysis of the consequences of military intervention in the process of development. It is, however, necessary to establish a conceptual link between the two if we are to advance a theory. Bienen remarked that when we understand reasons for military intervention and are able to explore the link between the military and other political institutions and social groups, we can better assess the prospects for the future evolution of the military in society and can better judge their capacity to deal with specific problems. He argued that the factors which explain military intervention also reveal the military's political capacity.[26]

Needler argued about the consequences of military regimes by examining the dynamics of military coups. He asserted that since the military is not always a homogeneous organization, the political viewpoints of military groups can be ascertained by examining the internal dynamics of coups.[27]

1. A coup is not made alone since outsiders are involved for advice and justification. This point is strengthened by the findings of Zolberg, who asserts that a large portion of the unexplained variation in military intervention is due to outside promptings and influence.[28]

2. Conspirators have varying orientations and objectives. Among these, the position of those who have the greatest outside support is strengthened. It has been argued that there were pro-East and pro-West factions in the Ghanaian military and that the pro-West faction (Africa group) won because of greater foreign support (this was not substantiated).[29] The subsequent reversal of the policies of the first military government by the new military government clearly attests to the existence of more than one orientation.

3. Autonomy to intervene may be reduced by the prevailing political situation. Lieutenant Colonel Ojukwu (subsequent leader of secessionist Biafra) and others planned military coups to coincide, among other reasons, with periods of greatest internal disturbance. Military interventions took place at a period of peak unrest in the country (October 1965-January 1966; May 1966-August 1966).[30]

If the military, or a particular group within it, seizes power because it has a specific program for modernizing society, then we are more likely to be able to adequately understand military performance as a governing group. Theoretically, if the military makes a coup with the aim of protecting or fostering some social interest, it probably has given some thought to the mechanisms by which this goal will be attained. The argument is not that the military has a detailed program, but that it possesses some king of orientation toward dealing with social or political forces. As such, the military has a greater capability than men who intervene in terms merely of corporate, professional interests.[31] Those who seize power primarily to preserve military-corporate interests will be forced, simply because they have succeeded in seizing power rather than through a choice of their own, to confront varied political forces and complicated societal problems. Since they have no prior orientation to these problems, they are likely to be indecisive, contradictory, and make ad hoc decisions in political and economic development.[32] Price clearly showed that the first military government in Ghana seized power to protect military-corporate interests, but bungled in political and economic decision making throughout its regime.[33] Declaration of intention is not proof of motivation, but the Nigerian military has demonstrated firmer control of the social order and greater enthusiasm for economic development (as revealed by the economic indicators) than did the multiparty system.

Military motivation to rule may not always be primarily significant in determining military performance. Changing political and social forces may alter the course of events to such an extent that the military is forced to alter its own plans in responding to such changes.

JANUARY 1966 AND JULY 1966 COUPS

The January 1966 coup was organized by a small group of majors (most of them peers in military training schools). Organizationally, this group was tight and highly cohesive. Peer group relationships were reinforced by the fact that all except one of the majors were Ibos, the majority ethnic group in the then Eastern region of Nigeria.

The small size of the army (10,000 men and 500 officers) was important in ensuring that the coup, which was organized by a tiny clique of majors, would succeed as far as it did. This was hardly likely to have happened in a much larger military establishment such as Nigeria presently has, with about 175,000 men and more than 2,000 officers (see Appendix 1). The progress of the majors' coup was halted when the head of the Nigerian army organized a successful resistance to the original coup. Therefore, the military junta that organized the coup was not the one that came to rule.

The original junta (members of which were arrested) had a clear political program, albeit a simplistic one. The spokesman for the original group, Major Nzeogwu, said in an interview: "We had a short list of people who were undesirable for the future progress of the country or who by their positions at the time had to be sacrificed for peace and stability."[34] In a subsequent interview on British television, he said: "We wanted to get rid of rotten and corrupt ministers, political parties, trade unions and the whole clumsy apparatus of the federal system."[35] Apparently, a clear sweep of the existing system was to be made before their definite program was to be launched. Essentially, the political hegemony of the north was to be destroyed and the basis of power altered.

Their program of political reform included the elimination of corruption, bribery, and embezzlement, and more important, the establishment of a strong, united, and prosperous Nigeria. They themselves did not intend to rule but wanted to handpick a handful of politicians who they considered honest enough to govern. These politicians were to have embarked upon a program to unite the country, although the specific mechanism for achieving such a lofty goal was not defined.[36]

The counter-coup, organized by General Ironsi, did not have any specific ideas about what to do, except to carry out a mandate from the outgoing civilian cabinet, which was to try to prevent the nation from crumbling. Ironsi's regime made a series of political mistakes, including the abandonment of a federal system of government and the institution of a unitary form of government. This step was followed by promotion within the military ranks, which, for whatever genuine administrative reasons they were made, appeared to the people as nepotic and favoring the Ibo ethnic group. These steps reinforced the already widespread notion that the coup was originally intended to promote Ibo domination. These fears resulted in a vendetta against Ibo people in May and led Ironsi to make further mistakes.

It is obvious that the coup which tore the nation apart in the first instance was not the one from which the leadership of the nation emerged. The lack of any program of rulership by the leadership of the coup within the coup cannot be laid at the feet of the original junta; indeed, the course of political development of the nation would have been different if the original junta had ruled.

Many events in the July 1966 coup which ousted the Ironsi regime (and from which the present leadership emerged) paralleled the events of the January coup. The army size had not increased; indeed, the officer corps had reduced in size. the coup was organized by cohorts of captains and lieutenants, not from a particular ethnic group, but made up largely of northerners displaying the well-known northern solidarity. It had the primary aim of returning the balance of power to the north and, thereafter, to secede, if possible, from the federation. Another similarity with the January coup was that it was not the original junta which staged the coup that is now ruling the country. The political atmosphere at the time was confused and fluid. The junta demanded that an officer of northern origin be named head of the nation. It appeared the junta itself did not intend to rule but to create political instability of such dimensions that their terms had to be accepted, although this cannot be firmly asserted. Lieutenant Colonel Gowon was the most acceptable at the time by virtue of his northern origin, his seniority, his ethnic minority status, and his Christian background. He accepted leadership only on the condition that he would be given a clear mandate by the junta to reunite the nation.

Having observed the mistakes of the Ironsi regime, Gowon immediately proceeded to restore the federal system and put in motion a series of constitutional meetings designed to restore normalcy. Although these did not succeed in uniting the nation (since the Eastern region finally seceded and became Biafra), the efforts to create stability and reunite the nation continued unabated. One of the results was the creation of states which became the cornerstone of renewed efforts to achieve stability. It is quite possible that the nation may never have remained united had the original July junta ruled the country (since they would have proceeded to pull the north out of the federation).

The events analyzed reveal that the performances of the military cannot be adequately evaluated without an analysis of the dynamics of the coup. Moreover, the deliberate attempts by the Gowon regime to avoid the mistakes of the Ironsi regime showed the ability of the military to learn on the job and adjust to the contingencies of the political situation.

NOTES

1. Huntington, S. P., *Political Order in Changing Societies* (New Haven, 1968). Nordlinger, Eric, "Soldiers in Mufti: The Impact of Military Rule Upon Economic and Social Change in Non-Western States," *American Political Science Review* 64 (1970): 1131-42.
2. Horowitz, Irving Louis, *Three Worlds of Development* (New York: Oxford University Press), ch. 12. David Apter, in his *Choice and the Politics of Allocation* (New Haven: Yale University Press, 1971), states that "the greater the degree of modernization, the greater the need for coercion," p. 42. His conclusion was based on evidence from Ghana, Uganda, and Latin America.
3. Needler, M., "Political Development and Military Intervention in Latin America," *American Political Science Review* 60 (1966): 616-26.
4. Huntington, *Political Order*.
5. Nordlinger, "Soldiers in Mufti," p. 1133.
6. Feld, M. S., "Professionalism, Nationalism and the Alienation of the Military," in J. A. van Doorn, ed., *Armed Forces and Society* (The Hague: Mouton, 1968), p. 68.
7. Deutsch, Karl, "Social Mobilization and Political Development," *American Political Science Review* 55 (1961): 4934.
8. Rustow, Dankwart, "The Vanishing Dream of Stability," *AID Digest* August (1962): 13.
9. Riggs, Fred, "Bureaucracy and Political Development: A Paradoxical View," in La Palombara, ed., *Bureaucratic and Political Development*, (Princeton, 1963), p. 139.
10. Almond, G. and Verba, Sydney, *The Civil Culture* (Princeton, 1963).
11. Hoselitz, Bert and Weiner, Myron, "Economic Development and Political Stability in India," *Dissent* 8 (1961): 172-79. Also, Olson, Mancur, "Rapid Growth as a Destabilizing Force," *Journal of Economic History* 23 (1963): 529-52.

12. Taylor, Charles L., "Communications Development and Political Stability," *Comparative Political Studies,* 4 (1969) 557-64. See also James C. Davies, "Political Stability and Instability: Some Manifestations and Causes, *Journal of Conflict Resolution* 13 (1969): 1-17; and A. Banks, "Modernization and Political Change: The Latin American and Amer-European Nations," *Comparative Political Studies* 2 (1970): 405-19. Pye, L., ed., *Communications and Political Development* (Princeton, 1963).
13. Hoselitz and Weiner, "Economic Development," 173-74.
14. Ibid.
15. Horowitz, *Three Worlds.* Apter, *Choice and Allocation.*
16. Huntington, *Political Order.*
17. Apter, *The Politics of Modernization.*
18. Klinghoffer, Arthur J., "Modernization and Political Development in Africa," *Journal of Modern African Studies* (1973): 1-19.
19. Zolberg, Aristide, "Military Intervention in the New States," in Henry Bienen, *The Military Intervenes* (New York: Sage, 1968), pp. 91-92.
20. Pye, *Communications,* p. 16.
21. Almond, G., *Political Development* (Boston, 1970), p. 190. Huntington, *Political Order,* p. 1.
22. Apter, *Choice and Allocation.*
23. Almond, G. and Powell, G. B., *Comparative Politics: A Developmental Approach* (Boston, 1966), p. 196.
24. The reason given for not discussing such issues as revenue allocation yet is because the necessary data, such as the new census figures which will permit meaningful discussion are only provisional. Encouraging open discussions until then will not only be a futile exercise but will also generate unnecessary controversial political discussion.
25. Bienen, Henry, "Public Order and the Military in Africa. Mutinies in Kenya," in his *The Military Intervenes,* pp. 35-70. Also his *The Military and Modernization* (Chicago, 1971). See also A. Zolberg, *Creating Political Order;* J. A. Coleman and Carl Rosberg, *Political Parties and National Integration.*
26. Bienen, Henry, ed., Introduction to his *The Military and Modernization* (Chicago, 1971).
27. Needler, "Political Development."
28. Zolberg, A., "A Decade of Military Rule in Africa," *World Politics,* January 1973.
29. Ibid.
30. *Government Printer,* Lagos, Nigeria, 1968.
31. Price, R. A., "A Theoretical Approach to Military Rule in the New State: Reference Group Theory and the Ghanaian Example," *World Politics,* October 1970, 399-429; and "Military Officers and Political Development," *Comparative Politics* 4 (1971), 361-79.
32. Ibid.
33. Ibid.
34. *Africa and the World,* vol. 3, no. 31, May 1967.
35. *West Africa,* London, January 22, 1966.
36. Kirk-Green, H. H., *Crisis and Conflict in Nigeria,* vols. 1, 2 (Oxford, 1971). See also H. Miner, *The Nigerian Army 1950-1966* (London, 1971); and R. Luckham, *The Nigerian Military: A Sociological Analysis of Authority and Revolt, 1960-1967* (New York, 1971).

Chapter 2
Theoretical Framework and Related Literature: Organizational Characteristics and Ideology of the Military in Nigeria

ORGANIZATIONAL CHARACTERISTICS

Traditional Structure of Coercion

Traditionally, the military is regarded as an institution which lays absolute emphasis on explicit orders, elaborate directives and well-laid-out contingency plans. Janovitz observed that its processes of communication and channels of command are characteristically pyramidal; that is, the distinctive feature of its operation is a downward flow of authoritative messages from the highest echelons of the hierarchy to the lowest other ranks.[1] In order to function effectively, the military requires a clearly defined channel of command, with adequate communications to ensure that orders are carried out and with means of disciplinary control.[2] Rapaport argued that this organizational strength to

15

carry out tasks characterizes the military: "Recognition of discipline in the army channels individual desires toward a common good. Secondly, an effective modern military organization requires a high degree of centralization. This feature emphasizes a high level of bureaucratic coordination necessary to achieve efficiency and control. That is, the military is assumed to operate essentially through a bureaucratic mode."[3]

The argument has been advanced that since centralization of power accords well with patterns of organization familiar to the military, the military, in organization terms, is a paragon of a modernized political system.[4] Such an assertion finds support in the work of other scholars who have equated modern government with centralization. Huntington said that:

> political modernization involves the rationalization of authority, the replacement of a large number of traditional relationships, familial, and ethnic political authority . . . . It means national integration and the centralization or accumulation of power in recognized law making institutions.[5]

Shils said that the military, because of the values of order and discipline, is a stable alternative to the party system.[6] Welch made the claim that few political parties in Africa can match the centralization, discipline, and communication of the smallest professional army on that continent.[7]

The main thrust of our argument is based, in part, on the rigid bureaucratic mode outlined above. It also rests, in part, on the transformed set of values that have developed as a result of structural changes in the military organization. The characteristics of hierarchy, order, discipline centralization, and bureaucratic coordination have been observed to change as a result of new technology and the demands of modern warfare, both in substance and in form. Flexibility and informal processes of communication are common; decentralization is replacing centralization of power; a more lateral and horizontal structure of command is replacing the older hierarchical structure.[8] In turn, the political process shapes and determines the character of military response and the military subsystem in general.

Emergent Organizational Characteristics of Military

The introduction of modern weaponry (such as nuclear warheads, new intelligence gathering mechanisms, etc.) into the contemporary military establishment has necessitated new training and the establishment of special branches.

First, the increasing complexity of the technology of warfare and the structural differentiation generated create the need for increasing coordination. Authoritarian discipline is hardly capable of coordinating such activities, and most modern militaries respond by developing lateral coordination and cooperation rather than by exercising the responsibility of higher echelons over the lower echelons.[9] Such developments are also found in the military of many developing nations and, in particular, Nigeria. Pye has noted the development of the signal corps and the engineering corps in the Burmese military.[10] The Nigerian military has undergone dramatic structural changes because of the civil war. In 1966, the military consisted only of an army of 8,000 men, and a very rudimentary air force consisting of four World War II trainer planes with about 90 men in the officer rank. In 1973, it had a fully developed military force of 250,000 men with several new or expanded branches (engineering, intelligence, education, signals); a new air force with several new officers; a new signal corps; and a navy (see Appendix 1). It is, of course, difficult to assert that structural transformations that are a few years old have significantly altered age-old orientations and attitudes, and that they have been responsible for the changes that will be described in the following pages. However, the peculiarity of the Nigerian situation (pluralism, high speed of development) and the dramatic and traumatic changes in the military (a new air force, a new navy, a new army — all new in size and hardware) require a process that will produce new men and new orientations adequate to cope with tense and fluid political conditions.

Second, the large increase in the recruitment of middle-level officers exacerbates problems of coordination and authority. Such proliferation creates the image that authority is being weakened since these officers "hold their ranks, not only on the basis of the number of subordinates they command but also because of their technical skills."[11] The introduction of such achievement criteria as skill (as opposed to seniority and age) has made status systems within the modern military more fluid and less clear cut.[12] This has resulted in a shift of emphasis from formal to informal mode of communication and therefore to persuasion; and to increased initiative, involvement, cooperation, and participation.[13]

The traditional forms of military command channels and communication processes by which authority, in the form of explicit orders, flowed downwards are giving way to informal processes marked by increasing prior notification of important decisions to all coordinate, lateral levels. The top levels of the authority system are also kept informed by elaborate informal channels. Janowitz asserted that the informal and unofficial channels of communication are "so important that they have become institutionalized in the oral briefings."[14]

The shift in emphasis from authoritarian control to more informal processes underlines the shift to initiative as a requirement of the modern military for effective operation. Since the combat unit is the organizational prototype of the military, the development of initiative at once becomes a more relevant and crucial variable in effective operation than an authoritarian enforcement of rules and discipline. Marshall has argued that the philosophy of discipline is adjusting to changing conditions. "As more and more power has gone into the hitting power of weapons, necessitating ever-widening developments in the forces of battle, the quality of the initiative in the individual has become the most praised of the military values."[15]

Janowitz had argued that the military establishment with its hierarchical structure, its exacting requirements for coordination, and its apparently high centralization of organizational power must always strive, contrariwise, to develop the broadest decentralization of initiative. In the same study, he noted that the contradictory interplay of practices designed to stimulate group initiative, and those practices which are required for organizational coordination are widespread contemporary bureaucratic processes.[16] Exactly how these apparently conflicting processes of centralized authority and decentralized initiative, force, and persuasion are employed in juxtaposition to one another will be analyzed in the following pages.

The decentralization already noted and the increasing emphasis on initiative must be accompanied by commitment on the part of the officers. An important aim of the military is the generation of involvement at all levels in the hierarchical structure. Involvement induces participation which, in a cyclical way, enhances chances of successful operation. "Thus as older forms of domination become outmoded, effective participation becomes a new criterion of judging military authority . . . and as the military authority shifts from emphasis on practices rooted in authoritarian domination, it moves to greater and wider employment of manipulation."[17]

It has been demonstrated that coercion, as traditionally conceived, has declined as the dominant mechanism of control in the modern military. The characteristics of cooperation, participation, manipulation, and persuasion appear to have given added flexibility and maturity to the military capability to maneuver in difficult political bargaining situations. This new situation accords well with situations in Nigeria, where (as will be seen later) the military as a bureaucratic organization, conceived of and born according to western bureaucratic ideals, faces the problems of rule in a largely traditional and plural society. The theoretical questions that political sociology faces, however, follow. (1) To what extent are such military organizational characteristics successfully applicable to other types of collective effort, particularly civilian political processes? (2) Are such characteristics sufficient to rule effectively?

Interplay of Political Processes and Military Response

Stepan has argued that no one factor, organizational or otherwise, taken in isolation can effectively explain or predict military performance. Once the military is engaged in civilian politics, we can no longer apply ideal-type organizational characteristics. The ideal military establishment, with a highly cohesive organization and its own set of codes and values, isolated from the vagaries and pressures of the political system, no longer exists. By means of consistent political interaction with the civilian polity, the military organization is both shaped by and shapes the political system of the society in which it is located.

Organizational characteristics, while very important, do not fully determine patterns of action on particular issues. The military often has various courses of action open to it at any one time and the choice of a course of action is, to a great extent, related to events within the political system itself.[18] Abrahamson argued that military officers are subject to pressures and expectations much as civilian politicians are (especially because they are part of a small elite leadership). The more a profession is exposed to such pressures, political or otherwise, the more, he argued, likely it is to choose strategies on the basis of both anticipated outcomes and professional ethos — rather than on organizational characteristics alone.[19] Since the political role of the military officers is expanding, they will become dependent upon an increasing number of pressure groups and will adjust their political roles to the needs and contingencies of dayto-day bargaining and ad hoc alliances with other groups. That is why, in this study, we emphasize the emergent military organizational characteristics and elements of political bargaining, such as persuasion and compromise. The structure and function of the military are related to the structure of politics at the time. While organizational characteristics are very relevant and important, the central task of political sociologists is to analyze the organization of the military and political system, and thus be prepared to show the manner in which the organizational characteristics of a particular military shapes its response to pressures emanating from the political system.

Constraints on Nigerian Political Process: Relation to Military Organizational Characteristics

Here we will discuss specific constraints on the Nigerian political processes in relation to organizational characteristics above.

The first and most central constraint on the pattern of Nigerian politics is pluralism (ethnic, religious, elite-mass, rural-urban). Ethnic pluralism has created a pattern of subnational conflicts unknown in any African nation. The military cannot effectively rule without due regard to the problems of equity and fairness among the various groups, while attempting at the same time to keep national interests in focus. It has to give local initiative to state governments (based as they are on ethnic affinities), while simultaneously ensuring uniform application of national policies. It cannot will away problems by simple and direct commands. The Nigerian military has superimposed its organizational structure on the polity (as described earlier). Ultimate power is centralized in the supreme military council and the federal cabinet (which consists of civilians), but each state cabinet (composed of military governor, military officers and civilian commissioners) exercises considerable initiative over certain areas. The requirement to take account of both initiative flowing from the states and the special demand of minorities places great stress on the use of force. The military, therefore, has had to also rely (as the specific example below will illustrate) on its ability to generate compromise by persuasion and to induce cooperation. It must be remembered, however, that the presence of force and its likely application are always lurking in the background. Such knowledge is by itself probably sufficient to induce the amount of cooperation necessary to produce results.

In organizational theory, this is similar to the force of authority in, say, a business corporation, where the ability to apply sanctions often underlies processes of bargaining between management and the employees. This, of course, is a two-way phenomenon and can operate in a cyclical fashion in such an interactive exchange situation. That is, while the employee recognizes the applicability of the management's sanctions and is therefore ready to cooperate, the management also appreciates that the employee could apply sanctions by withdrawing services. That constrains either party in applying sanctions. This tacit but delicate interplay of power is disrupted when one party actually applies sanctions in order to enforce its demands. The extent and scope of such applied sanctions depend on the perceived ability of one or the other party to strike back. In military rule in Nigeria, where the military establishment and civilian polity are the two parties in an exchange situation, the power possessed by both are not of the same quality. The military has the power of physical force, while the civilian polity can mobilize public opinion and force military governments to resign.[20] It is hardly logical and probably irrelevant, therefore, to argue whether they are equal or not. The lack of direct application of military force is an important factor in inducing quiescence in the people.

What generally happens in the Nigerian situation is that the military issues orders and threatens to back them up with physical force only after negotiation and persuasion have failed. In such cases where it has laid down explicit orders beforehand (for instance as in the military decree prohibiting trade strikes), it has often reneged and bargained first. That is, it has not physically prevented strikes but has directed the parties concerned to negotiate. Where it is directly involved as an employer, the military has showed a willingness to negotiate. Rather than a sign of weakness, this is a response to political demands, as well as a mature attempt to cope with potentially unstable conditions in Nigeria. It appears that the military establishment itself has continually learned the art of political bargaining so necessary in order to govern successfully.

The military government ostensibly came to power to ensure that political stability was maintained and economic progress made. When General Gowon came to power, the nation was undergoing such turmoil that the only alternative to complete disintegration was the establishment of a strong unifying government. Its subsequent actions appear to have confirmed these objectives. In contrast to the Ghanaian situation, the government of General Ankrah had assumed power to serve military corporate interests. It had no clear program and worse still, was hampered by corporate motivation in its efforts to rule. It bungled from one political mistake to the other and finally collapsed.[21]

In general, the ideal typical military approach of coercive force as a mechanism of control appears to have been tempered in Nigeria by flexibility in political bargaining. However, not every nation under military rule adopts this approach. Brazil has a modern military with certain new developments described above, but it is hardly a flexible ruler. Cases of torture, repression, and a general orientation toward coercive force are very common, and even pervasive.[22] Our explanation for the difference between the two countries lies in the characters of their political processes. Brazil is less pluralistic and more advanced economically. Therefore, the kind of bargaining and maneuvers necessary for political stability may be different, although this is not to imply that political bargaining is more or less necessary in the one nation than in the other.

In recently instituting national service for all university graduates, the Nigerian military more than once changed the structure of the program to accommodate demands contained in protests, while insisting that national service was essential, logical, and rational. The military was prepared to back this up with force if need be. Thus, it emphasized rational policies and tried to accommodate initiative and dissension alongside of them. An admixture of bureaucratic modes of coordination (order, discipline, hierarchy), infused with flexibility that derived from compromise and persuasion, operated in such spheres of military governmental activity as economic development and modernization. It was reflected in the formulation and manner of policy execution, as we shall see in the following analysis of selected policy areas.

Handling Foreign Investments. The federal military government is moving to reduce dependence on foreign aid, and this affects policy making regarding the proportion of capital that foreign interests will be permitted to invest. Problems are created for foreign investors and the different states alike because of differential inducements offered by the states. The policy dilemma raised for the federal military government is how to coordinate the varying needs and financial abilities of the different states with those of the investors in a centralized policy that reflects uniformity of purpose and avoids duplication. The government set policy guidelines, by which any state government must own at least 35 percent of the shares of any new or old project. This policy did not exist during the multiparty regime—a condition that resulted in unhealthy rivalry and consequent exploitation of observable regional differences by the foreign investor. This minimum base line of 35 percent allowed each state enough room to maneuver. Rich states could invest up to 50 percent or more, and the range provided for limited competition among the states. The competition is healthy, in the sense that it gives the poorer states impetus to work toward the generation of capital necessary for participation in project investment. If, however, a state is unable to mobilize enough capital to match the basic minimum, the federal government may offer financial aid. While investment policy is centralized to allow for more uniform application than in prewar times, enough scope is allowed for initiative and competition.

Handling Location of Federal Projects. One aspect of economic development which is closely related to political stability is the siting of federal industrial projects. Conflicts arose in prewar days among different ethnic groups during political lobbying for industrial projects. These reinforced separatism and posed political problems of unity and legitimacy. This tended to put ethnic group claims over those of the nation and, thereby, cast doubts on the legitimacy of the nation. How has the military government allocated resources in such a way that no one group is completely alienated?

"Resources" refer to any state of affairs that is desired by any one person or group of persons, or to generic commodities available in the polity.[23] Resources are "divisible." The government can increase, decrease, promise, or limit the availability of a resource. Resources are rarely permanent. If a petroleum refinery is to be located in the Rivers state of Nigeria, it must have minimum capital and size of operation, but if the government is interested in providing a cheaper source of power and fuel (which is a generic policy question), it may allocate natural gas or hydroelectric power. Thus, people interested in getting projects located in their areas may get industrial projects of different sizes and dimensions of operations. That is, within certain policy areas, the government has an appreciable degree of freedom to maneuver to reduce any given aspect of any given policy. Resources used as reward variables by a government can be divided into units or slices which, in effect, make them continuous. The government is not faced with the difficulty of choosing between either giving out such reward variables or not giving them at all. It can parcel them out. Conceiving of resources as continuous variables makes it easy to evaluate to what extent the multiparty system and military regimes have effectively used resources to maintain stability.

The multiparty system was permeated by ethnic demands of such great intensity that it had to either locate a project in one place or shelve it altogether, as happened in the case of the iron and steel industry. The most powerful ethnic group got the most resources, and this, coupled with the cumulative requirement of vertical industrial integration, ensured that resources were concentrated in a few areas. When one region got an industrial project (for a nonrational economic reason), it insisted that, for economic rationality (that is, reducing costs of distribution and transport of usable products), new industries requiring its byproducts be located near it. Political obscurantism, based on nonrational ideas, employed rational reasons to support itself; the ethnic group took precedence over the nation. While we are not even now underestimating the influence of powerful lobbying, the military system has attempted to disperse the resources by dividing them as much as possible. The military has placed the idea of nation over that of the ethnic group. At the same time, however, it has taken account of what sites are most logical and rational. If one group was making noises about the need for a certain project, the military government offered another slice of the pie. The state or ethnic group usually accepted this, appreciating that if they rejected the offer there might not be another one. Such a group usually does not want direct confrontation, because they fully realize that the military owes no special obligation to them as a specific constituency and has the power to enforce its decisions. In the few years of rule, the military has established a greater measure of authority and legitimacy than the multiparty system did. The next section will examine the nature of this authority and the peculiar problems of legitimacy that it poses.

AUTHORITY AND LEGITIMACY

Problems of national integration and modernization in Nigeria make the establishment of a strong government inevitable.[24] A strong government needs authority to rule effectively and African governments have failed essentially because they lack authority. What is the nature of authority as we refer to it here? What is its source? How well accepted can it be? What makes the military's system of authority more or less effective than that of the party system?

In sociological literature, the definition of authority cannot be considered apart from the notions of legitimacy and power to act. Weber's analysis of authority is based on the concept that action in a system must be coordinated and oriented to an order which must be carried out and enforced by a responsible agency. This is the concept of "imperial coordination," and it means that certain specific commands from a given source will probably be obeyed by a given group of persons. Weber's typology of authority (rational, legal, traditional, and charismatic) rests on the claims of each type to legitimacy.[25] Parsons contends that authority is the "institutionalized code within which the use of power as a medium is organized and legitimized. It is the aspect of a status in a system of social organization by virtue of which the incumbent is put in a position legitimately to make decisions which are binding not only on himself but on the collectivity as a whole . . . in the sense that so far as their implications impinge on their respective roles and statuses, they are bound to act in accordance with these implications."[26] Parsons elaborated further that this includes the right to insist on such actions as the incumbent may deem fit (a notion that carries with it the threat of force). Legitimacy, according to Parsons, defines the right of participation in the power system. Authority can, therefore, be seen as a set of rights in status, including the right to acquire and use power in that status.[27] Odegaard sees authority as "compliance motivated by attitudes towards legitimacy," and thus, his definition lacks the element of force in extracting such compliance.[28] Odegaard is supported by Fried,[29] who contends that authority is the ability to channel the behavior of others in the absence of threat or sanctions. Such definitions as the latter two are imprecise, for the reason that the meanings of "force," "threat," or "sanctions" are not identified. Even simple routine exchange situations in which authority relations are involved (as, for instance, between the employer and the employee bargaining over wages) carry the threat of sanctions, as described earlier.

Friedrich sees authority as the acceptance of the fact that certain individuals or offices possess the right to rule.[30] Dahl defines it as the influence of a leader clothed with legitimacy.[31] Both political scientists are concerned with legitimacy and both are also imprecise in demarcating the extent to which "force," "threat," or "sanctions" are applicable variables to the generation and sustenance of authority.[32] The relationship of force, power, threat, or sanctions to the meaning of authority (so poorly defined in most of the literature) seems crucial if "authority" and "legitimacy" are to be linked conceptually. Can we argue, for instance, that the colonial government, which imposed and maintained its rule (for a long time) by force of arms and threat of trade and commercial sanctions on African nations, was not a legitimate government? The answer is "no." Because it had ruled effectively over a long time, the colonial government was accepted as legitimate; nobody would now look back to the beginning of colonialism with whatever hindsight and declare that that government was illegitimate. Force or threat or sanction as a mechanism, therefore, cannot be considered independent of the time element in analyzing its relationship to authority. If Ian Smith's government in Zimbabwe (Southern Rhodesia) succeeded in entrenching itself in power either by silencing all opposition or producing all the goods required to satisfy the people's expectations, questions of its illegitimacy over time would be weakened. Is the South African government illegitimate? It appears, therefore, that analysis of authority as a goal and the mechanism of achieving that goal have a crucial intervening variable—time—which determines whether authority has been achieved or not. This is not to underemphasize the importance of the acceptance and understanding that a government is right, moral, or ethical.

In Parsons's definition and in general sociological literature, time is instrumental in institutionalizing a position or status. In Parsons's definition of authority as "right in status," time has defined or crystallized status through institutionalization.[33] In the emergence of a new status such as leadership, effective management of the status is crucial; without it, the status is disregarded by the society. Whether, at the very outset of rulership in new nations, a government is legitimate or not is a less important question than how effective a government is. In contemporary international diplomacy, a new government that may have been installed by force is recognized by others (who themselves eschew the use of force) and is accepted as legitimate if it shows authority by exercising effective control over time. A prime contemporary example is Greece. Authority, therefore, is a phenomenon that exists only in relation to time. The authority of an old institution becomes questionable if it becomes progressively less effective over time. The ruled accept a government as legitimate to the extent that it satisfies their needs, that it is effective, and that it shows authority. The acceptance of certain individuals or offices as possessing the right to rule is dependent on their effectiveness over time.

Dahl defines legitimacy as "the belief that structures, procedures, acts, decisions, policies, officials, or leaders of government possess the quality of rightness, propriety or moral good and should be accepted because of this quality."[34] But this definition appears narrow. It prohibits the determination of the relative degree of legitimacy of a nation's political institutions. One thus loses a key variable in analyzing the stability of those institutions when they are faced with a crisis of effectiveness. That is why it was not possible for political sociologists to determine whether the

Nigerian, Ghanaian or Sierra Leonean governments were becoming more or less effective, since they were initially legitimate governments. When, in time, is this belief in qualities of "propriety," "rightness," and "moral good" acquired? Lipset's idea, that legitimacy is the capacity of a political system to engender and maintain the belief that existing political institutions are the most appropriate ones for the society, appears broader and more comprehensive.[35] He argues, in other words, that the extent to which a government can be accepted as legitimate is dependent on the extent to which it practices norms and builds institutons shared by the majority of the people. The relationship between legitimacy and authority is indeed dynamic. We cannot say whether a government or type of governing is legitimate except in reference to the time, circumstance, and place in which it is situated.

A crucial theoretical question in relation to the political sociology of Nigeria becomes: how is the military converting its power to authority? To what extent, are people making "noises" that may undermine the emergence of its legitimacy and acceptability? The Nigerian military government is trying to earn legitimacy through a number of mechanisms: (1) building effectiveness over an extended period of time and creating institutions that will outlast them; (2) creating social bases of support and avoiding excessive resort to the use of force; (3) using various leadership styles such as charisma, patrimonialism, and the symbolic uses of politics; and (4) stressing, military ideologies of nationalism, national unity and cohesion, and modernization as "symbolism" to inspire and to rule.

Building Effectiveness Over Extended Time Period

Lipset[36] asserted that prolonged effectiveness may lend legitimacy to a government by constant economic development; Horowitz,[37] and Cutright and Wiley[38] emphasized that the relationship between military determinism and high economic growth tends to be stable over time precisely to the degree that civilian mechanisms are found wanting. There are a few propositions here that lend themselves to formalization.

1. Constant economic development leads to prolonged effectiveness (Lipset).

2. Prolonged effectiveness lends legitimacy to a government (Lipset).

3. There is a positive correlation between military rule (mechanisms) and high economic development (to be high, it must have been constant over time, Horowitz).

4. There is, therefore, a positive correlation between military rule and prolonged effectiveness (prolonged in the sense that economic development is constantly high and increases for a reasonable length of time).

5. Thus, military governments (who may have intervened forcibly and therefore illegitimately) may earn or acquire legitimacy through prolonged effectiveness. There is, however, very mixed evidence on the ability of the military to achieve high economic development. Nordlinger believes that the military is incapable of achieving economic development and cites several examples.[39] He is supported by Price, who showed that in Ghana's first military government, the military was quite incapable.[40] But Horowitz has found that in some countries, notably Brazil (since 1964) and Argentina, the military has performed well.[41] It appears that the military's ability to rule must be determined case by case. Military capacity to rule effectively cannot be abstractly generalized (which is what many writers have done) but must be related to factors such as the social and political structure of the society concerned, the motivation to intervene, and the capacity to learn political bargaining on the job.

In short, the relationship between authority and legitimacy is dynamic, since with acquired legitimacy, authority increases, and with increased authority, legitimacy is advanced. Chapters 6 and 7 will demonstrate that the Nigerian military government has achieved prolonged effectiveness over its duration of rule (in terms of economic indices of production, growth, and structural differentiation). The multiparty system ruled for slightly under six years after independence, during which time the above indices were significantly lower than those achieved by the military.

Creating Social Support and Avoiding Excessive Recourse to Force

Sociological literature has consistently emphasized the need for the military to establish a civilian base of support for its policies (Janowitz,[42] van Doorn,[43] Bienen,[44] Zolberg,[45] Nordlinger,[46] Halpern,[47] and Levy[48]). Yet the political sociology literature abounds with statements to the effect that the military is incapable of generating such support. Bienen asserted that the military is unable, due to its conservative nature, to develop instruments that will generate grass roots support,[49] and Nordlinger has argued that the military is unlikely to be motivated by goals of popular responsiveness, social or economic reforms, or economic development.[50] While it is true that, ideally, the party system does reach the grass roots, the military also has a political style. The military in Ghana, Dahomey, Congo, and so on have established a liaison with the people by means of special advisory councils. These councils perform the crucial function of bargaining for substantive resources, as well as fulfilling the symbolic function of a group of experts planning on behalf of the people. The Nigerian military government established several such councils which have performed successfully.

Zolberg has argued that one effective instrument that governments in emerging countries can establish to reach the grass roots is a corps of dedicated men and women whose duty it is to explain governmental policies, programs, and activities.[51] Nigeria has recently done this, although it is too soon to properly evaluate its effects.

A critical factor is the ability of the military to remain cohesive, which, in turn, depends on several factors, one of the most important of which is the quality of leadership. A military in politics needs to develop a leadership cadre that not only enjoys the loyalty of most of the officers and other ranks but also the support of the nation. Nasser, Boumédienne, and their top hierarchies demonstrated the ability to control both the military and the people.

The military can achieve such support by civilianizing itself, as in the cases of Ataturk and Nasser, in part. But what are leadership qualities? How are they employed in Nigeria? In our discussion of the military leadership style in Nigeria, we shall emphasize theories of charismatic legitimation, the concept of patrimonialism, and the symbolic uses of politics and military ideology used as symbolism in the search for legitimacy.

Leadership Styles: Charismatic Legitimation, Patrimonialism, and Military Ideology as "Symbolism"

Because political leadership is subtle, difficult, and complex, its dynamics and processes can be best analyzed from characteristics of individuals and responses of the led. Charisma and patrimonialism, and more importantly, the responses elicited from the masses are critical factors. The masses are controlled through manipualtion of their wants, and through externalization of their anxieties by mechanisms such as inspirational, hortatory rhetoric pertaining to nationalism, puritanism, modernization and national unity.

Our main premise is that leadership conveys meaning and that the meaning thus conveyed is a central explanation of political stability or polarization.[52] Bennis has argued that governmental leaders have tremendous potential capacity for evoking an emotive, strong response in large populations.[53] Edelman has asserted that differences between two political leaderships do not depend on differences in policy directions but on leadership styles.[54] He emphasized that leaders increasingly rely on style differences to create and emphasize an impression of maneuverability. The impression remains an important political fact, although maneuverability may not. The crucial point is how effective the response of political groups is in particular situations. Very often, the clue which helps masses perceive what is politically effective does not reside in the verifiable good or bad effects of political acts, but in whether the leadership exhibits the capacity to convey the impression that they know what is to be done.[55] In Nigeria, the civilian political elite, prior to January 1966, demonstrated that it did not know what to do at the federal level. The regions became small nations and the prevarication of the federal political leadership (as in their ambivalence in handling the Western Nigeria political crises of 1962, their inability to act on the census of 1963, their inept handling of the general strike of 1964, and the breakdown of law and order in Western Nigeria in 1965) reflected the ineffectuality of the political leadership.

Since the assurance that the leadership knows what to do is so intensely sought by the masses, this will predictably be attributed to the leadership group whose activities "can be interpreted as beneficent, whether it is because they are demonstrably beneficent or because their consequences are unknowable."[56] A leadership like the military which exhibits competence in handling problems of political stability, national sovereignty (the civil war), and economic development becomes acceptable on its own terms. The military has not only taken dramatic steps to allay the fears of the minority and to integrate the country, it has more consistently coordinated economic development plans than did the multiparty system. In addition to any concrete, substantive results it may have achieved in this direction, the military has, at the very least, created the illusion or symbolic impression that planning of the nation's future and consequences is possible to a far greater degree than it may demonstrably be.

The essence of the leadership style already described is neither charismatic nor bureaucratic leadership.[57] The main elements of this style are not rational, routine, and determinable results, and, therefore, the style is not bureaucratic. The key elements depend on mass assurance, not on routines to determine decisions. Nor does the military's leadership style depend on extraordinary personal qualities like those of a charismatic leader. It depends, at least in the case of mutually hostile groups in government on a disinclination to upset the apple-cart. Sometimes, it even depends on the failure to demonstrate success or failure, and on the disposition of the alienated masses to project their "psychic needs upon the incumbents of high office."[58]

Let us illustrate with examples from the United States and Nigeria. Gallup polls revealed that Eisenhower, Kennedy, and Johnson all maintained consistently high ratings throughout their administrations, except when they took decisive actions that caused harm to particular groups. In Nigeria in 1962, the federal political elite rocked the boat by intervening decisively in favor of a particular group in a political dispute in Western Nigeria. This action constituted an important link in the chain of events that led to the civil war. Again in 1963 and 1965, the federal political leadership hurt specific groups in conducting the population census and the local regional election in Western Nigeria. The military, in contrast, has avoided taking firm positions on certain highly controversial issues that may cause irreparable harm to specific groups. In the dispute between the Ibos of East Central state and the Ibiobios of the Rivers state (Port Harcourt), the federal government has issued a decree, in general form, urging each state to return the properties of those who have fled. But the return of the Ibo property in Port Harcourt would mean the return of almost the entire city, the capital of the Rivers state, to Ibo people. (Both ethnic groups were part of secessionist Biafra.) Thus, a direct command in either direction would harm one side. At the time of this writing, this issue was the most controversial one in communal integration among both groups in Nigeria. General Gowon has avoided an authoritative position, but has encouraged local negotiations and stated that he hopes good sense will prevail. Rather than employ authoritarian mechanisms of control, the military can be flexible in managing complex civilian politics.

Another controversial issue is the federal allocation of revenue, a primary source of political instability in Nigeria. Action on arriving at a definite formula has been postponed pending the completion of the population census. A formula might have been reached based on the controversial 1963 census, but this would have resulted in instability. The present ad hoc procedure amounts to an attempt to buy time, during which hostilities would subside to some extent, a volatile subject would be shelved temporarily, and the basis for a new formula might be created.

Avoiding an authoritative position on a controversial issue, while at the same time appearing as a protagonist against an ever-present bogey or enemy (in the Nigerian case, lack of unity), helps to retain or increase political support from large numbers of antagonists on both sides of a controversy. The political leadership can maintain symbolic leadership through ascriptions of their ability to cope or through publicized action on noncontroversial policies. Hyman and Sheatsley, commenting on Eisenhower's nonaction on a controversial issue, said: "Eisenhower's lack of commitment at this time simply encouraged his supporters to see him either as a non-partisan leader or as an unspoken sympathizer with their own views."[59] In the Nigerian case, both the East Central and Rivers states peoples are likely to perceive General Gowon as a nonpartisan leader.

The military leadership is not always ambivalent. It has been forceful, courageous, and decisive on many issues. The military has, however, achieved a better combination of active and passive governing roles than did the civilian political elite. Paradoxically, the military, traditionally considered authoritarian and rigid, has shown as much political bargaining ability, flexibility, and resilience as the civilian political elite. Such ability as the military has shown has led influential weeklies such as *West Africa* magazine, which consistently monitors political events in West Africa, to comment that the Nigerian military government is more resilient, more tolerant, and far more conciliatory than the civilian leadership.[60] The military ostensibly assumed a leadership role to put "things right," and with a dedicated leadership such as Nigeria has at present, the awareness of that role and its duties are kept constantly in view. During civilian rule, the leadership was heir to the political struggle for national liberation and, hence, regarded it as their sacred right to share what is characteristically known as the national cake. It is quite possible that if the military stays in power too long, it may begin to believe it has performed a wonderful duty which demands ample rewards and compensation.

The contrast in leadership styles reinforces Weiner's assertion that it may not be the form of political system in emerging countries (authoritarian, democratic, military) that is important, but the quality and ability of the leadership to respond to the needs of the masses.[61]

Charismatic Legitimation Versus Patrimonialism as Explanatory Tools

The charismatic theory of legitimation suggests that one mechanism by which individual political loyalties are transferred from parochial to ecumenical levels is by means of a charismatic leader, whose special appeal to a people differing in a number of respects (ethnic, religion, class) is widely accepted. This notion relates to legitimacy, in the sense that it helps as an important transitional phenomenon to advance political integration. We shall deal with the works of five theorists: Wallerstein, Weber, Horowitz, Runciman, and Ake.

Wallerstein noted that West African governments do not hold the residual loyalty of most of their citizens. His argument rested on the fact that political integration takes place only when the citizen accepts the state as the legitimate holder of force and authority, and the rightful locus of legislation and social decisions. For Wallerstein, the main instruments for legitimating the state are the dominant political party and the charismatic leader. (It must be noted here that he was referring to the one-party states of the Ivory Coast, Mali, Ghana, and Tanzania.) Wallerstein further posited that recognition of the authority of the state is facilitated if the state's claims are put forward by someone who the masses trust and respect. That is, the masses revere the leader in a way that they do not respect the state, and the charismatic leader's authority can be used to buttress the state until it wins legitimacy. "The charismatic justification for authority can be seen as a way of transition — an interim measure which gets people to serve the requirements of the nation out of loyalty to the leader while they do so for its own sake."[62]

Apter's approach contains considerable insights into the structure and processes of Ghanaian political life. He found that the Ashanti confederation was characterized by an observable separation between the individual and his office, limited functions of authority, and a hierarchic administrative structure. The political transfer of western political institutions did not totally disrupt the traditional society, since elements of the traditional social structure were compatible with the bureaucratic system. However, he observed that political institutional transfer is potentially disruptive. One element that can sustain society under the consequent stress is the emergence of a nucleus of unity. The leader's charisma derived from the fact that he fulfilled the functions of the chieftaincy and met the chief's functional requirements. The leader also acted as a symbol referent. In this way, Nkrumah appropriated the authority of the chief, and "as charisma has worked . . . as a newly accepted source of legitimacy, it has provided for the public extension of legitimacy and support to new types of social structures in keeping with the objectives of nationalism, meanwhile retaining sub-relational aspects of the traditional system, and integrating these aspects in different relational and behavioral modes permissible by Nkrumah's sanctions."[63]

Weber's classical concept of charisma[64] has been criticized in several respects. Blau noted that Weber's theory "encompasses only the historical processes that lead from charismatic movement to increasing rationalization and does not include an analysis of the historical conditions that give rise to charismatic eruptions in the social structure."[65] Even though social change and rapid transformation are largely unsettling and create ripe conditions for charismatic politics in Nigeria and elsewhere in the third world, we cannot make the conceptual jump that such a setting leads to alienation and charismatic politics. The lack of clarity of the historical conditions that lead to charismatic politics highlights some of the logical problems inherent in the use of Weber's theory.

Friedrich observed that charisma does not provide an adequate type of leadership, but only of power. He further noted that leadership presupposes the existence of structured power (institutionalized power), but charisma is the very antithesis of structured power. Thus, it is not clear what charismatic leadership means.[66] Emmett commented on the narrow conceptualization of Weber's typology because Weber assimilated it too hastily to a personal and irrational kind of authority.[67]

Relating these general critiques to the African condition, we find that Apter's functional analogy of the charismatic leader to the chief may be misleading. Assuming that Nkrumah appropriated the authority of the chief, would that make him acceptable to the average Ghanaian citizen as the source of authority? What differences in structure and processes determine people's responses? Ake noted that political functions have been performed through different structures.[68] Almond states that the sophisticated functionalist will note that the kinds of structures that man the boundaries of the political system do matter, since it is these structures that process the "inputs" and "maintain the contact between polity and society."[69] Ake points out that it makes a difference politically whether civic disorder in Alabama is checked by the local police or by federal government troops.[70] Of course, it matters whether tax collection in Nigeria is undertaken by the akodas (vassals) of the Olubadan (King of Ibadan) or by the law enforcement agents of the state.[71]

The problem in Nigeria is complicated because there is not one traditional political system but several (ranging from the Hausa, to the Yoruba, Ibo, Bini, and Kanuri). No single national political party system embraces the whole society. The emergence of one charismatic leader was difficult in the face of such ethnic and religious divisions. Azikiwe was by far the most acceptable (probably charismatic) leader in the days before independence, but the situation changed dramatically with the competitive ethnic politics of the postindependence era.

Runciman, however, argues that the routinization of charisma was taking place under Nkrumah.[72] He asserted that the Convention Peoples Party, as a symbol of unity which transcended persons and the incarnation of the aspirations and the interests of the people of Ghana, was replacing Nkrumah's waning charisma. Support for the tendancy to regard the dominant party as the instrument for routinizing charisma can be found in Horowitz's work. Pointing out that the third world exhibits contrasting trends in extralegal authority and legal-rational authority, Horowitz noted that personalism existed side by side with bureaucratic organization (the party). Horowitz argued that these antithetical tendencies have been synthesized in party charisma. The shift in the functions of charisma after the struggle for national liberation was brought about as a result of pressure towards synthesis. In the postrevolutionary era, charisma tends to become depersonalized in the effort to create order and stability. He asserts further that "time-honored distinctions drawn by Max Weber between the three ways to legimate authority, through traditionalism charisma and rationalism tend to draw the distinctions more tightly in theory than they are in fact."[73]

In Runciman's and Horowitz's work certain methodological questions remain unanswered. How can we identify routinization as a process in party development? Are not the dominant parties of the third world instruments of reinforcing the authoritarianism of the leader rather than instruments of routinization? Nkrumah became increasingly athoritarian, instead of emphasizing bureaucratic development of the party.

It is true that Gowon came from a minority ethnic group and was, therefore, acceptable to the feuding majority ethnic groups; he is also a

Christian (son of a church minister), which increased his appeal in southern Nigeria. His northern origin endeared him to northerners. His humble origin and achievement of elite status in the military earned him an across-the-class appeal. He is the hero that led the nation through a most difficult war and set it on the road to unprecedented economic development and political stability. While these qualities are important enough to make him a charismatic leader, they may not necessarily lead to the acceptance of the military government as having authority and being legitimate and effective. Party politics and military politics do not develop along the same lines, and the notion of charisma has not done much to explain postindependence politics, either civilian or military. The concept of patrimonialism is much more fruitful than the notion of charismatic leadership. Zolberg argued that, although charismatic political leadership prevailed during the struggle for national leadership in Africa, the present style of leadership in one-party states appears more patrimonial than charismatic.[74] Roth also argued that in the new states of Africa and Asia, patrimonial elements far outweigh charismatic appeal. Roth further claims that the neglect of patrimonial elements has led scholars to interpret all political leadership as charismatic, thereby obscuring the difference between a charismatic system of authority and charismatic leadership.[75]

Patrimonialism as Leadership Style

Patrimonialism, according to Weber, includes elements of patriarch-alism and traditional authority.[76] The civilian politicians used these means to appropriate public office as the prime source of status, prestige, and reward. Political and regional fragmentation based on the exploitation of primordial sentiments by respective ethnic leaders resulted. The employment of the same ideas by the military could also lead to fragmentation, if the military was factionalized. But then, it would no longer be one military. Clearly, a crisis of authority had existed in Nigeria (as in many other emerging nations of Africa and Asia).

The same crisis hardly existed when the chief (the Emirs, Obas, Obis) had a significant hand in governing during colonial times. The colonial rulers worked through the chief (especially the northern Nigeria indirect rule system) but, in general, established viable local governments all over the country. Wraith concluded that the politicians, after independence from Britain, took the introduction of European democratic institutions as license to curtail the power of the chiefs.[77] They ambivalently expected the chiefs to maintain law and order in their domains, but systematically deprived them of the power to do so.

What are the bases of authority for the average Nigerian? It can be argued that the Nigerian who naturally accepts the authority of an Oba or

Emir will readily follow the authority of a colonel, but that the acceptance of the authority of a politician by the same citizen, unless that politician is a patriarchal figure (for instance, Leopold Senghor of Senegal), will depend on the politician's performance — a performance which rarely matches his promises. The politician is usually distributed, whether or not his failures can be temporarily concealed by appeals to ethnic or other passions. The secularization of authority requires a shift in loyalty. Once in Nigeria and twice in Ghana, military rule was greeted with genuine enthusiasm, and this illustrates how fickle political loyalty is. Except for Gambia, democratic civilian institutions have very shallow roots in West Africa. According to Horowitz, the military, in general, seems to be performing better in the specific areas of establishing law and order and promoting economic progress than did the civilians.[78] If we are not to see anarchy in Nigeria or elsewhere in West Africa, on what basis can authority be established? Certainly not through a charismatic leader: the Institute of Administration at a Nigerian university conducted a research survey and concluded that, in the permanent task of government in the villages or even in the transition from military to civilian rule, the chiefs still have a major role.[79]

The crucial question is not whether an average Nigerian will accept the authority of a colonel because he has naturally accepted that of a chief. Both work within different institutional structures and, therefore, have different output and impacts. The point is whether the position of the chief is different under the military from what it was under the civilian political system. The chiefs, according to the findings of this institute, had to curry the favor of the politicians or the ruling party — a situation that tended to destroy them. When the military came, the chiefs, working through the civilian bureaucracy, were able to strengthen their authority. Some theoretical explanations can be advanced to explain this situation:

1.   The military, being dependent on the civilian bureaucracy, took the bureaucracy's advice. Of course, being a traditional British creation, the civilian bureaucracy had worked with and thoroughly understood and respected the capacity of the local chieftaincy and government.

2.   The military, being a conservative institution and, simultaneously, lacking the direct means of ruling, preferred to work through the chiefs. The military has come in as a father figure, dusting up old institutions and creating new ones. Perhaps this apparently paradoxical quality has made it essentially capable of fulfilling the role of governing in Nigeria (however transitional it might be). The military is using patrimonialism as a neotraditional mechanism of reaching the people. Does the military, so closely identified with bureaucratic and modern authority, revert to traditional authority in the manner in which Weber classified authority? The answer is yes. The appeal to the masses of the people from a

patriarchal, patrimonial vantage point is more logical in a plural, divided, and traditional society. The Ibos of secessionist Biafra are hardly likely to accept Gowon as a charismatic leader. But an assumption of a father-for-all posture is likely to be more palatable than a hero figure. Gowon and his top officers are therefore employing neotraditional and cultural appeals more effectively than the party leaders did.

The evocation of the ideologies of nationalism, unity, puritanism, and modernization may find more ready ears than the inspiration from a charismatic leader. In sum, we are making the following observations.

1. The concept of patrimonialism is a more adequate tool for the explanation of postindependence politics than is charisma.
2. The civilian political elite, because of the ethnically competitive character of postindependence politics, employed patrimonialism as a mechanism to grab political office, political spoils, and patronage.
3. The military has used patrimonialism in a more patriarchial (more Weberian) sense — that is, acting as father figure, arbiter, and conciliator among feuding groups. However, we cannot dismiss the fact that some members of the military have been as corrupt as the politicians they replaced. The redeeming feature is that such officers, when and if detected, have been publicly punished: shot by a firing squad. Therefore, differences exist in the way both leadership groups have attempted to govern and relate to the people.

The patrimonial tendencies of the military are fusing with the increased bureaucratization of society. Just as Horowitz and Runciman suggested a routinization of charisma through party development, so are we suggesting a routinization of patrimonial tendencies through military bureaucratization. The military elite legitimizes itself in office by the dual processes of patrimonial and bureaucratic legitimation. The fusion first emerges because most of the patrimonial, patriarchal appeals are issued through official bureaucratic channels. A major example is the military system in the Middle East where, according to Shlomo, political modernization takes the form of appeals to a traditional Islamic culture. "Within the Arab context, the emergence of military regimes has signified a reversion to the traditional legitimate form of government accepted and revered by the Arabs and by Islam for the past 1500 years . . . within the political culture of the Arab society, military power equals political legitimacy and for this reason, military leaders have had very little difficulty establishing their authority in Arab countries."[80] Levine observed that the Ethiopian military has a self-confident realization that it is the only institution that is simultaneously traditional and modern, and that it has a national mission to procreate the new national culture of modernizing Ethiopia.[81] This is also true of Nigeria, Algeria, and the Congo. In Libya, Qaddafi is basing his contemporary cultural revolution on the Koran,

Islamic teaching, and puritanism.[82] The above examples further justify Horowitz's claim that the distinction drawn by Max Weber between the three ways to legitimate authority tend to draw distinctions more tightly in theory than they are in fact.[83]

Most of the political institutions which are considered traditional today first appeared in colonial times. Zolberg has said that, "tradition does not merely refer to pre-European times. Many political institutions created during the colonial period have become, in the eyes of the living men, part of the natural order of things; district commissioners, provincial commissioners, commandants . . . are offices hallowed by time. The African occupants of these offices derive their authority from the fact that they are legitimate successors to the original charismatic leaders."[84] "Tradition," as it applies to bureaucratic institutions, is drawn from recent history, and most of Nigeria's recent history is one largely of bureaucratic, paternalistic structures. We have employed the term tradition in two different senses. In one sense, tradition refers to time-hallowed ancient cultural norms and structures — forms which the military has used in a neotraditional sense (much as used by the displaced political elite). This will become clearer as we elaborate on the use of military ideology below, and in a later chapter dealing with economic nationalism. In the latter sense, tradition implies preservation of and respect for institutionalized bureaucratic structures which have become the bulwark and mainstay of governments in times of crisis. Such respect and attempts at preservation are reflected in the intense conservatism of the civilian bureaucrats themselves, some of whom (in what is an ordinarily trivial but sociologically significant sense) preserve the appurtenances and prerequisites of office of the departed British colonials. The inherently bureaucratic structure of the military itself, its bureaucratic approach to policy and problems, and its respect for order and systematic progress attest to its orientation toward bureaucratic coordination.

The dependence of the military on the civilian bureaucratic system underlies the increasing bureaucratization of society. The civilian bureaucratic system serves an analogous function to military leadership, as the party does to the civilian political leadership. James Coleman, analyzing nationalism and social structures in emergent countries, commented that experience has shown that the authoritarian rule of the military, in conjunction with a civilian bureaucracy, is not an ephemeral arrangement; indeed it may be a substitute for party government. In the same article he suggested that the army and the civilian bureaucracy are alternative elites, committed to growth, unity, and stability.[85]

Whether or not the military-bureaucratic arrangement is an ephemeral one, there are points of commonality which are worth exploring. There appears to be a set of ideas held in common by the young officers and by large sections of the civilian bureaucracy. Even though military training is not an exact copy or complement of civilian experience, Janowitz holds that skills are transferable to middle-level civilian administration.[86] Certainly, sufficient model patterns of experience exist to ensure sympathy between the two groups. Primary socialization and education patterns, and the structural position of the bureaucratized military vis-a-vis the politicians are also similar.

Because both the bureaucracy and military were organized in colonial times into relatively rigid hierarchies with limited scope for initiative and relatively ordered promotion (although conditions are changing in both institutions), they have conservative attitudes. They both evince firm interest in ordered modernization and economic growth. Both are well-placed to get what the politicians failed to get.[87] The bureaucracy and the military both benefit society at large.[88] Both can enter into coalitions to further their own interests or defend them when attacked.

Symbolic Uses of Politics: Military Ideology as "Symbolism"

Nordlinger avidly criticized the military of the third world countries for indulging in empty rhetoric designed to serve no purpose when they intervene in politics.[89] It is true that all military juntas present themselves as reformers. Nasser proclaimed that the "military must end the exploitation of the people, realize national aspirations, raise the standard of living of the masses, expand education and develop national consciousness that is an indispensable preliminary for a sound democracy."[90] The Nigerian military also proclaimed that "the military has come to bring an end to gangsterism and to disorder and corruption and nepotism."[91] Rustow offered the following generalization. "In the mid-twentieth century, any serious claimant to power, regardless of his antecedents, associations or intentions, will justify his claim by professing profound concern for national independence, for popular aspirations, for social justice and for economic development."[92] Hurewitz claimed that "at the hour of the political triumph, all army officers in the post-war Middle East have claimed to be card bearing reformers."[93]

Nordlinger interprets the officers' initial assertions as pretentious, claiming that as soon as they have seized power, these officers are unlikely to be motivated by goals of popular responsiveness, social and economic reforms, or economic development. The weakness of Nordlinger's interpretation stems from his belief that only concrete and substantively verifiable success can sustain political stability. While it is true that concrete results are necessary, they are by no means sufficient, taken as a unit, to create stability. As we have been trying to demonstrate, the use of symbolism is associated with political quiescence, and it is an indispensable ingredient in producing results.

Political quiescence by the masses concerning an area of policy can be assumed to be due to either lack of interest, or to "the satisfaction of whatever interest the quiescent group may have in the political question."[94] When people are faced with such stressful, anxiety-ridden, complex, and ambiguous situations as Nigeria faced during and after the civil war, people respond massively to reassuring symbols. In fact, these symbols may be oversimplified and distorted, but the extent to which reality can become irrelevant for persons very strongly committed to the need to satisfy emotion has been well-documented.[95] Emotional commitment to a symbol is associated with contentment and quiescence, with reference to issues that would otherwise arouse concern. What Nordlinger overlooked in his criticism is that the way social images are manipulated can make it possible for members of a society to believe that they live in a well-organized and good society.[96] While civilian politicians are capable of manipulating the populace (and this is what they do most of the time), the military also does it, perhaps to an even greater extent. For how could Nasser have held the attention of the Egyptians and controlled them for so long with minimal concrete achievement, without symbolic manipulation?

The difference between civilian and military political leaders is that military leaders have more concrete ideologies to throw around symbolically, and sometimes do so in a somewhat more articulate, more forceful, and more incisive manner than does the civilian politician. In Nigeria, it was not apparent that civilian politicans ever evolved an ideology that could be symbolically used for political ends. What was most evident was division among them and lack of an integrated perspective or orientation. While the military itself may be divided on several issues, its organizational characteristics make expression of common ideological principles possible.

Military and civilian rulers are also dissimilar in the language forms, or combination of language forms, which they employ to induce quiescence. The military has always sought to expound its own ideologies in order to justify intervening in politics. It has also employed various forms of language to propagate these ideologies to the polity in the attempt to induce a sense of commitment and political quiescence, and carry the populace towards a common national goal. The military is not always committed to lofty national goals, however. In the following pages we shall focus on the following points.

1.   The military portrays itself as the embodiment of nationalism, national unity and cohesion, puritanism, and modernization.

2.   While the military may not necessarily be truly nationalist, puritanical, cohesive, or modern, such a portrayal serves the symbolic functions of systematically reassuring the masses and inducing political quiescence.
3.   Military politicians employ this method more than do civilian politicians in Nigeria through various combinations of the above language forms.

Ithiel de Sola Pool argued that the importance of political language is not accuracy but the appraisal common to members.[97] The Nigerian military attempts to bring a divided people together, in part by the use of consciously expressive symbolic rhetoric that has universal appeal. Edelman claimed that the generation of evocative symbolism involves a corresponding diversion of attention from cognitive and rational analysis and manipulation of the environment.[98] Since the civil war, there has been a deliberate attempt at conciliation and trends toward the use of terms that evoke a common nationality, unity, stability, economic progress, and puritanism.

If a people have common faith in a symbol, it compels attention, causes emotional release and compliance, and also promises to heal anxiety. The Ibos of former Biafra were intensely nationalist and were, to some extent, in the vanguard of liberation struggles before national independence. Even before 1966, political acts emanating from this ethnic group were no less nationalist than those from any other. Fears of ethnic security are being allayed by intense conciliatory efforts and by deep appeals to a symbolism in which these people have for so long believed. The aim of such symbolic appeals, in general, is to legitimize specific future acts, the content of which may be unknown, and thus to maximize the chances of acquiescence and compliance with what they embody.[99] The military may not itself be nationalistic, puritanical, cohesive, or modernizing. There is intense controversy over whether the military (especially in the third world) possesses any or all of these qualities. The focus of the discussion is on the relative ability of civilian or military politicians to establish political stability by the invocation of these ideologies. The outlines of the controversy are substantially as follows.

Ideological Qualities of the Military

Janowitz said that the most central and pervasive of the ideologies of the military are nationalism and puritanism. He argued that, "At the core of these themes is a strong sense of nationalism and national identity, with pervasive overtones of xenophobia; in varying degrees this outlook applies to the military as a profession. . . . A second and widespread element is a strong puritanical outlook. This again seems to be a rather universal characteristic of the military."[100] Finer said of the military: "Its whole espirit de corps without which it would have no fighting spirit is founded on the supposed heavy emphasis on the national identity and whips up patriotism and nationalism in its recruits."[101] Halpern said that the Middle Eastern armies are "committed to nationalism and social reform . . . they have served as national standard bearers . . . within the army, a sense of national mission transcending parochial, regional or economic interests or kinship ties seemed to be much more clearly defined than elsewhere in society."[102] Pye asserted that the army is an unambigous symbol of national authority,[103] while Levy holds that the military harbors radical feelings about the status of the nation as a whole.[104]

The counter-argument asserts that foreign agents of imperialism penetrate the nation through the military. Third world militaries, because of their structural dependence on the metropole for arms and other goods, are never able to espouse true nationalist standards.[105] Price amply documented the antinationalist politics of the first Ghanaian military regime. He also showed how widely unpuritanical the first Ghanaian military was.[106] There is evidence that many Nigerian officers have been found to be corrupt. But the military has sought to maintain its image by publicly executing such officers.

The Nigerian military has, however, recently displayed nationalism to an extent that western analysts consider excessive. It has given more military and financial support to liberation movements in the continent than has any other African nation. It has moved in the direction of strong economic nationalism for the nation. It has also sought to discourage unions that have strong ethnic flavors; that is, it has encouraged nationalist patriotic feelings.

Some scholars have argued that the military is the most modernized and refined organization in the third world, because it is imbued with rational norms.[107] On the contrary, Bienen argued that it is not correct to say that the argument for the military as a modernizing force rests on the proposition that military groups have more modern attitudes and are more advanced than the civilian elements.[108] This may be the case in some areas (for example, the Middle East), but it is certainly not the case in many former British West African states where the civilian bureaucracy was stronger than any other institution.

Is the military itself substantively cohesive? Because of its organization, the military is characterized as a melting pot "in which various heterogenous elements are united."[109] It is an organization which can draw "recruits from all tribes and regions in the state and give them the same training and experience."[110] The military is an arbitrary social group in which position and relation are determined by criteria of military rank and proficiency rather than by preservice status.[111] But it should not be assumed that membership in a heterogenous army necessarily fosters a national outlook. Evidence shows that recruitment to African armies is so skewed that it is difficult to say the military diminishes ethnic rivalry. Lee commented that the African military has broken down exactly at those points at which the rest of the polity showed signs of stress (for instance, the second military uprising in Nigeria reflected the internal ethnic division of the country).[112] Horowitz aptly commented that the sensitivity of military institutions to political and class (let us add, ethnic) cleavages makes them as much a part of the problem as a part of the solution.[113] The Nigerian situation appears exaggerated, however, and taken out of context.[114] In the first military uprising, officers from a particular group commanded men of another ethnic group. This was ample illustration of a military ideology of cohesion transcending ethnic, primordial loyalties. The internal cohesion of the military broke down only after the first coup, following what is now widely recognized as partisan policy and planning of the Ibo general who took over power after the first coup. The unusually frequent consultations among military leaders, the consistent pursuit of the common goals of reconstruction, stability, and economic development, the obvious trust, respect, and confidence in its leadership has given, at the very minimum, an outward appearance of cohesion to the present Nigerian military.

The fact that the Nigerian military exhibits, in some measure, some of the elements of the ideologies earlier described gives it added encouragement to seek to unify the nation through these ideologies. We emphasized earlier that the expression of these ideologies is no empty rhetoric — they perform symbolic functions. Edelman argued that, of the possible meanings of a political language style inherent in its structure, the researcher identifies its actual meaning for a particular public by observing their response to it.[115] The methodological question is: what are the formal properties of political language which may correspond to observable responses of interested publics? Edelman identified four styles: hortatory, legal, administrative, and bargaining, all dealing with authority, persuasion, and participation; that is, whether people see themselves as ultimately ruler or ruled, included or excluded.[116]

The hortatory style, focusing on appeals to particular audiences for policy support, is directed toward the mass audience. The connotations of its contents are usually notoriously ambiguous and consist of premises which may denote outside threat to the people. Indeed, whether or not the people of Nigeria agree with nationalist appeals for stability, in spite of the ambiguity of such terms each occasion when this language is used is taken by the people as evidence of widespread support of public policy. When Gowon visited the East Central state (heartland of former Biafra) with hortatory appeals for national reconstruction, conciliation, and stability, he was widely received and acclaimed. However, while the premises of the reasoning may be disputed (here was an apparent victor speaking to an apparently conquered people), the assumption that such an appeal is necessary (because of the need to conciliate), and the fact that the public response will influence policy, is taken for granted and is strengthened by every serious response.[117]

Mutual cuing of evocative connotations may establish an aura around a sign, so that intensity is lent to the response.[118] Thus, when Gowon says that Nigeria must now command the towering heights of its own economy; when after Biafra received clandestine support from several nations, he declared publicly that Nigeria now knows who her enemies are; when speaking in support of African liberation movements, he asserts that Nigeria has a leading role to play in liberating all of Africa from the yokes of imperialism,[119] the term "nationalism" acquires a meaning out of all proportion to the user's original intentions. Economic nationalism generates support from traders, businessmen, and labor unions who suspiciously eye foreign enterprises; a cry for liberation makes him the rallying focus of all nationalist elites.

Nigeria is pictured as a great pan-African nation, liberating the rest of colonial Africa and trying to bring the rest of independent Africa together in a united front against neocolonialism. This is similar to Nasser's effort to lead the Arab nations and, at one time, to lead the rest of Africa. It is comparable to Qaddafi's current efforts to lead the Arab world.

Military regimes distrust interest groups or individual men who are protecting their own specific interests, because they may represent threats to the nationalist aims the regime is espousing.[120] One of the rationales often used to justify a military coup is that it was undertaken to stop greedy, selfish men who have corrupted the nation. Implicit in this is the assumption that there is a divergence between the claims of the community. The military is in a difficult position if it openly emphasizes such differences, especially because men will not trust those who have been in power for a long time, but also because men always seek after their own gain. The military has to present its ideologies in forms that reconcile such divergent claims. This is done, on the one hand, through propagating the ideology of nationalism, an ideology that embraces the larger community; and, on the other hand, by propagating some form of socialism, as in the encouragement of public enterprise, an ideology that promises better life for the peasant.

The common goals of the nation — political stability and economic development — espoused by the military can be achieved through industrialization and agricultural improvement. These two mechanisms promise better living standards for the peasant or the urban proletariat. Any persons who frustrate these goals are enemies that must be overcome. This is the context in which such symbols are continually put and which may eventually induce an automatic response. The overcoming of such enemies constitutes a form of purification.

In Nigeria, the public exposure of corrupt men and the execution of armed robbers and corrupt military officers constitute ritual acts of regeneration. These rituals are designed to bind people together in a common ideology of puritanism. "An ideology can bind rulers and the ruled, and myths and utopias can give the military coup and its regime scope and dimension."[121] It is seen then that ideology can help the military lay claim to higher goals which are highly symbolic in themselves and can provide the moral basis for manipulation to those ends. The massively positive response of the masses to public executions would have been horribly incomprehensible without such a theoretical explanation.

If Nasser did not achieve very much by way of substantive improvements, he did strongly reinforce Arab nationalism, just as Perón established a political base of power with Argentinian labor. What is significant is that both men attempted to and succeeded in associating specific symbols with goals they had in view, and propagated the symbols to achieve those goals. Nasser wanted Arab expansionism and peddled nationalism. Perón so effectively symbolized his regime with the use of ideologically inspiring expressions — *justicialismo,* the dignification of labor, the humanization of capital, and so on — that his followers won another election in Argentina after 17 years of Perón's exile. Thus, "the characteristics of symbols serve to give common political language to those who share them and make their practices coherent. They provide a common means of communication without requiring precise definition."[122]

Nigeria, more than ever, needs the articulation of coherent ideologies to unify its peoples. Independence and national liberation ideologically unified the people during the colonial struggle. Perhaps the ideologies of nationalism, puritanism, socialism, and modernization can serve as rallying foci to unite the same peoples today.

Forms of Language to Express Ideology

In the responses they continually make, affected publics declare their confidence that valid logic and adequate data will guide political agencies to reflect the people's values and other universal norms.[123] This will hold until confidence in the government has been dangerously eroded. To sustain the level of enthusiasm with which it was received at its accession to power, the military government continually emphasizes these ideologies. The constant employment of the hortatory language style is accepted as evidence that the Nigerian public has a stake and role in political decisions. Therefore, a formal appeal for support is made for the manner of rule being adopted because it is logically demonstrable that national unity, nationalism, puritanism, and modernization will serve the widest public, directly or indirectly — that the meaning and content of political language reinforces the tendency toward a quick response to political activities and events.[124]

Besides the hortatory form of language, the military uses a legal-administrative language style which comes in the form of decrees. This combines precise definition, carries command and authority, and creates an impression of a kind of executive supremacy. This accords well with earlier emphasis on the employment of military organizational characteristics of order and authority in rule. But along with this is the employment of the bargaining style. In an effort to gain support for a policy position, the government, as a bargainer, offers a deal, not an appeal. This is reflected in the division of resources and the use of persuasion and compromise earlier described. In the bargaining situation, a public reaction is to be avoided, not sought. The specific mechanisms that the military has employed in the bargaining posture are the establishment of interstate agencies or commissions. To the masses, the propaganda attending their establishment and the publicity given to their recommendations constitute recognition of the need for bargaining. To the military, as well as to civilian politicians, bargaining catalyzes governmental procedures. When bargaining is in process, the view that the public interest is being carefully safeguarded by experts is being manipulated. Examples in the United States are the deliberations of the National Security Council. On a more global scale, the supreme military council of NATO or the supranational ministerial council perform similar functions.

Certainly in Nigeria, the National Defence Council, the National Economic Commission, and a host of other organizations established during the military regime (some established earlier have been given duties and reinforced) are helping to shape the procedures of the military government. The dependence of the military on civilian bureaucratic procedures is a phenomenon that gives it strength.

The privacy and secrecy that pervade the working of such agencies induce public misconceptions about the extent to which negotiation is involved. Edelman argued that such misconceptions involve assumptions that bargaining is safeguarding a wider public, when in fact this may not be so.[125] These agencies work systematically (as we will demonstrate in Chapter 3), which constitutes another instance of a meaning, conveyed by form, promoting social harmony and quiescence. Since legal, administrative, and bargaining styles occur simultaneously with hortatory styles in the contemporary Nigerian political scene, it is easy for the masses of the people to underestimate the bargaining and administrative styles (the two by which resources are really allocated), and to overestimate the importance of the hortatory style (the one that conveys symbolic reassurance) for resource allocation. Indeed, it appears that the most important function of the hortatory form is to assure a mass public, in order to make it easier for groups that are directly involved to perform their functions effectively and freely in the later policy-making stages.

In this chapter, we have sought to convey the impression that quiescence concerning political goals is largely a consequence of various forms of symbolic reassurance. If certain types of political goals are not satisfied symbolically, they are more likely than not to erupt into direct, extragovernment mass action. Of course, symbolic reassurance alone is not sufficient, and in the following chapters we shall describe the provision of the concrete demands.

We also do not wish to leave the impression that only the military is capable of employing these various combinations of styles. The shift in emphasis from pre-independence ideological struggle to more rational postindependence governmental planning, the failure of the civilian political elite to achieve just that, the unhealthy political competition based on ethnic rivalry, and the highly plural character of Nigerian society forestalled the emergence of a coherent political ideology capable of performing a symbolically reassuring function.

Military organizational characteristics and different political styles of the civilian and military elites can be summarized as follows.

1. The military political elite has the command and authority resources to promote development in a more forceful, direct manner and to induce political stability through coercion, persuasion, and compromise.
2. In a plural independent society, patrimonialism takes the place of charisma.
3. The military employs patrimonialism to relate to the people (in a patriarchal form) while the civilian political elite uses patrimonialism competitively to grab public office. While the military use of patrimonialism leads to cooperation among various units of the plural society, civilian use always tends to cause territorial and political fragmentation. However, this distinction may not be so marked in a society that is homogeneous.
4. The military combines various forms of political symbolic reassurance to induce quiescence and stability by means of ideology expressed in the combination of language styles, such as hortatory, legal-administrative, and bargaining. The ideological repertoire of the civilian political elite is not quite so rich. While the civilian elite can use these forms in equal measure (a decree is equivalent to an executive order, and both can be backed up by the use of force) military organizational characteristics of command, cohesion, and hierarchy make these forms more easily applicable in a plural society.

The failure of the multiparty system in Nigeria and the one-party system in Ghana may have been highlighted as a result of the peculiarly plural nature of the Nigerian society, or the failure of Nkrumah to reach down to the grass roots. The military in Nigeria may not always perform better than the multiparty system, but in their present transitional role, they have shown capability, flexibility, and skillful use of bargaining skills. In this respect, the military has demonstrated its ability to guarantee national sovereignty, and promote stability and economic development.

The military's efforts in substantive problem and policy areas (such as integration, power distribution, and economic development) will be elaborated upon in the following chapters.

NOTES

1. Janowitz, Morris, *Sociology and the Military Establishment* (New York: Sage, 1959); *The Military in the Political Development of New Nations* (Chicago, 1964). Janowitz, Morris and J. van Doorn, *On Military Intervention* (Rotterdam, 1971).
2. Ibid.
3. Rapaport, David, "A Comparative Theory of Military and Political Types," in S. P. Huntington, ed., *Changing Patterns of Military Politics* (New York, 1962).
4. Welch, C., *Soldier and State in Africa,* (Evanston, Ill., 1970), pp. 36-40.
5. Huntington, S. P., "Political Modernization: America versus Europe," *World Politics* 18 (1966): 378.
6. Shils, Edward, "The Military in the Political Development of New Nations," in J. J. Johnson, ed., *The Role of the Military in the Underdeveloped Countries* (Princeton, 1962).
7. Welch, *Soldier,* p. 36.
8. Janowitz, *Military Establishment.*
9. Ibid.
10. Pye, L., "The Army in Burmese Politics," in J. J. Johnson, ed., *The Role of the Military in the Underdeveloped Countries* (Princeton, 1962), pp. 331-352.
11. Janowitz, *Military Establishment,* p. 28.
12. Ibid.
13. Ibid.
14. Ibid.
15. Marshall, S. L. A., *Man Against Fire* (New York, 1947), pp. 22, 36.
16. Janowitz, *Military Establishment.*
17. Ibid.
18. Stepan, Alfred, *The Military in Politics: Changing Patterns in Brazil* (Princeton, 1971), p. 21.
19. Abrahamson, B., *Military Professionalization and Political Power* (Beverly Hills, 1972).
20. The case of Argentina in 1971-72 reflects such a situation.
21. Price, R., "A Theoretical Approach to Military Rule . . . "
22. The North America Council on Latin America has reported several cases of torture.

23. Curry, R., and Wade, L., *A Theory of Political Exchange: Economic Reasoning in Political Analysis* (Englewood Cliffs, 1968).
24. O'Connell, James, "The Inevitability of Instability," *Journal of Modern African Studies,* vol. 5, no. 2, 181-91.
25. Weber, Max, *The Theory of Social and Economic Organization* (New York, 1957), p. 363.
26. Parsons, Talcott, "On the Concept of Power," *Proceedings of the American Philosophical Society* 107: 232-62.
27. Ibid.
28. Odegaard, P. H., "A New Look at Leviathian," in L. White, ed., *Frontiers of Knowledge* (New York, 1956).
29. Fried, Morton, *The Evolution of Political Society* (New York, 1967).
30. Friedrich, Carl, *Man and His Government* (New York, 1963), p. 24.
31. Dahl, R., *Modern Political Systems* (Englewood Cliffs, 1963).
32. Ibid.
33. Parsons, T., "On the Concept of Power."
34. Dahl, R., *Modern Political Systems.*
35. Lipset, S. M., "Some Social Requisites of Democracy: Development and Political Legitimacy," *American Political Science Review* 53 (1959): 69-105.
36. Ibid.
37. Horowitz, Irving Louis, *Three Worlds of Development* (New York: Oxford University Press), ch. 12.
38. Cutright, Phillips, and Wiley, James A., "Modernization and Political Representations," *Studies in Comparative International Development* 5 (1969-70): 23-40.
39. Nordlinger, Eric, "Soldiers in Mufti," *American Political Science Review* 64 (1970): 131-42.
40. Price, R., "A Theoretical Approach to Military Rule . . . "
41. Horowitz, *Three Worlds.*
42. Janowitz, *Military Establishment; Political Development.*
43. Van Doorn and Janowitz, *On Military Intervention.*
44. Bienen, H., *The Military and Modernization* (Chicago, 1971).
45. Zolberg, A., "Military Intervention in the New States of Tropical Africa," in H. Bienen, ed., *The Military Intervenes* (Chicago, 1970); "A Decade of Military Rule in Africa," *World Politics,* January 1973.
46. Nordlinger, "Soldiers in Mufti."
47. Halpern, M., "Middle Eastern Armies and the New Middle Class," in J.J. Johnson, ed., *The Role of the Military in the Underdeveloped Countries* (Princeton, 1962).
48. Levy, M., "Armed Forces Organizations," in *Modernization and the Structure of Societies: A Setting for International Affairs* (Princeton, 1966).
49. Bienen, The *Military and Modernization.*
50. Nordlinger, "Soldiers in Mufti."
51. Zolberg, "Military Intervention."
52. Edelman, M., *The Symbolic Uses of Politics* (Urbana, 1967).
53. Bennis, G., "Leadership Theory and Administrative Behavior," *Administrative Science Quarterly* 4 (1959): 295-301.
54. Edelman, *The Symbolic Uses of Politics.*

55. Ibid., p. 74.
56. Ibid.
57. Gerth, H., and Mills, C.W., *From Max Weber: Essays in Sociology* (New York, 1958), p. 246.
58. Edelman, *The Symbolic Uses of Politics.*
59. Hyman, H.H., and Sheatsley, P., "The Political Appeal of President Eisenhower," *Public Opinion Quarterly* 17 (1953-54): 443-460.
60. *West Africa,* May 1972; January, March, and May 1973.
61. Weiner, M., "Political Participation and Political Development," in M. Weiner, ed., *Modernization* (New York, 1966).
62. Wallerstein, I., *Africa: The Politics of Independence* (New York, 1961), p. 87.
63. Apter, D., *Ghana in Transition* (New York, 1963), p. 18.
64. Weber, M., *The Theory of Economic and Social Organization.*
65. Blau, P., "Critical Remarks on Weber's Theory of Authority," *American Political Science Review* 57 (1963): 305-16.
66. Friedrich, C., "Political Leadership and the Problem of Charismatic Power," *Journal of Politics* 23 (1961): 3-24.
67. Emmett, D., *Function, Purpose and Power: Some Concepts on the Study of Individuals and Society* (London, 1958), p. 242.
68. Ake, C., *A Theory of Political Integration* (Illinois, 1967), ch. 4.
69. Almond, G., "A Developmental Approach to Political Systems," *World Politics* 17: 183-214.
70. Ake, C., *Political Integration.*
71. The Nigerian police are withdrawing their men from the duties of tax collection because of the disturbances that have followed such exercises. See *West Africa,* May and July, 1973. The duties will be performed by local men selected by local elders or chiefs.
72. Runciman, W.G., "Charismatic Legitimacy and One Party Rule in Ghana," *Archives Europeanes de Sociologie* 4 (1963): 148-65.
73. Horowitz, I.L., "Party Charisma," *Studies in Comparative International Development* 1 (1965): 84.
74. Zolberg, A., *Creating Political Order* (Chicago, 1966).
75. Roth, G., "Personal Rulership, Patrimonialism and Empire Building in the New States," *World Politics* 20 (1968): 199.
76. Weber, *The Theory of Social and Economic Organization.*
77. Wraith, quoted in *West Africa,* June 28, 1973.
78. Horowitz, *Three Worlds.*
79. Report issued by the Institute of Administration, Ahmadu Bello University, Zaria, 1972.
80. Shlomo, A., "The Palestinians and Israel," *Commentary* 49 (1970): 31-34.
81. Levine, D., "The Military in Ethiopian Politics: Capabilities and Constraints," in Bienen, ed., *The Military Intervenes.*
82. Qaddafi appears to succeed in inducing commitments to the Islamic cause from his people.
83. Horowitz, *Three Worlds.*
84. Zolberg, *Creating Political Order.*
85. Coleman, J. and Rosberg, Carl, *Political Parties and National Integration in Tropical Africa* (Berkeley, 1966).
86. Janowitz, *Political Development.*
87. Coleman, J. and Bryce, "The Role of the Military in Sub-Saharan Africa," in J.J. Johnson, *The Role of the Military.*

88. Blau, "Critical Remarks."
89. Nordlinger, "Soldiers in Mufti."
90. Nasser, G.A., "The Egyptian Revolution," *Foreign Affairs* 33 (1955): 208-9.
91. Miner, N., *The Nigerian Army: 1956-1966* (London, 1971), p. 177.
92. Rustow, D., *A World of Nations* (Washington, D.C., 1967).
93. Hurewitz, J.C., *Middle Eastern Politics: The Military Dimension* (New Jersey, 1970), pp. 419-37.
94. Edelman, *The Symblic Uses of Politics.*
95. Festinger, L., Riecken, H., and Shacter, S., *When Prophecy Fails* (Minneapolis, 1956).
96. Salamon, A., "Symbols and Images in the Constitution of Society," in L. Bryson, L. Finkelstein, H. Hoagland, and R.M. MacIver, eds., *Symbols and Society* (New York, 1955), p. 110.
97. Pool, Ithiel de Sola, "Symbols, Meanings and Social Science," in L. Bryson, et al., eds., *Symbols and Values,* ch. 23.
98. Edelman, *The Symbolic Uses of Politics.*
99. Ibid.
100. Janowitz, *Political Development.*
101. Finer, S.E., *The Man on Horseback* (New York, 1963).
102. Halpern, "Middle Eastern Armies."
103. Pye, ., "Armies in the Process of Political Modernization," in J.J. Johnson, *The Role of the Military.*
104. Levy, "Armed Forces Organization."
105. Horowitz, *Three Worlds;* Murray, R., "Militarism in Africa," *New Left Review* (1966): 37-57; McAlister, L., "Recent Research and Writings on the Role of the Military," in *Latin American Research Review* 1 (1966): 5-36.
106. Price, R., "Military Officers and Political Development," *Comparative Politics* 4 (1971), 361-79.
107. Levy, "Armed Forces Organization."
108. Bienen, *The Military and Modernization.*
109. Pye, "The Army in Burmese Politics."
110. Jordan, A., *Foreign Aid and the Defense of South East Asia* (New York, 1962).
111. Walterhouse, H.A., *Time to Build: Military Civil Action Medium for Economic Development and Social Reform* (Columbia, 1964).
112. Lee, J.M., *African Armies and Civil Order* (New York, 1969).
113. Horowitz, *Three Worlds.*
114. The assumption is usually made that Nigerian problems always arise from issues connected with ethnic pluralism.
115. Edelman, *The Symbolic Uses of Politics.*
116. Ibid.
117. Ibid.
118. Ibid.
119. General Yakubu Gowon, Speech at the OAU Conference, 1972.
120. Horowitz, *Three Worlds;* Fert, E., "Pen, Sword and People: Military Regimes in the Formation of Political Institutions," *World Politics* January 1973, 271-92.
121. Edelman, *The Symbolic Uses of Politics.*
122. Ibid.
123. Ibid.
124. Ibid.
125. Ibid.

Chapter 3
Political Development and Political Stability in Nigeria

The central question to be explored in this chapter is whether the military-bureaucratic system has built or fostered political development in a way that contributes to political stability. The specific dimension of political development to be focused upon is national integration (to be defined below). Secondarily, we will investigate what new institutions have been built, or how old ones have been reinforced, to perform the task of national integration; we will also investigate how these institutions have been built and how they are performing the task of integration.

The first step is to define empirically what we mean by national integration. Coleman and Rosberg defined national integration as subsuming two auxiliary processes: territorial integration, the progressive reduction of cultural and regional tensions and discontinuities, in the process of creating a homogeneous community; and political integration, the bridging of the elite-mass gap on the vertical plane, in the process of developing an integrated political process and a participant community.[1]

The above definition is eminently applicable to the Nigerian situation, where cleavages in the polity occur both at the horizontal level (communal or ethnic cleavages) and the vertical level (elite-mass and rural-urban gaps). Our concern here is with the following three aspects: (1) communal integration; (2) reduction of the elite-mass gap; (3) reduction of the urban-rural gap.

Conceptualizing integration as a process helps to lay the bases for making analytical propositions from empirical facts. Haas conceived of political integration as a process whereby political actors in distinct national settings are persuaded to shift their loyalties, expectations, and political activities toward a new center, the institutions of which possess or demand jurisdiction over the pre-existing nation-state.[2] Even though Haas was referring to the nations of Europe, his conceptualization has relevance for the many states or regions of Nigeria. Haas's definition can be interpreted to mean that political integration is the process whereby, for a certain number of political units, institutions are developed which can attract and support these units, and which can make these into binding decisions. That is, political integration comprises the institutions of a particular political process.[3] Etzioni conceived of integration as the extent to which a political system has developed certain decision-making capabilities. For him, it implies certain common organizations or institutions for the system as a whole.[4]

In further developing this point, De Vree argued that political integration is concerned with the way a political process comes to be ordered, regulated, or structured by means of decision-making institutions.[5] Because integration has to do with the creation and development of decision-making institutions, it is possible to evaluate integration in terms of the capacity of such institutions to make such decisions. We will be examining to what extent increased capacity has been generated by the creation of additional institutions or by the strengthening of old institutions. We are, therefore, conceiving of institution building as any increase of the decision-making capacity of the common institutions of some political system.[6] Such increases are made either accretively on the old institutions, or by the development of new ones to process the load of demands made on the old institutions. It can then be argued that the decision-making capacity of a political system is greater: (1) the greater the number of decision-making institutions; (2) the greater the binding force of the decisions among the political units (states in Nigeria); (3) the greater the amount and/or variety of the decisions (by variety is meant the number of sectors or issue areas touched upon); (4) the more significant or salient each political unit considers such decision areas to be.[7] To what extent, compared to the multiparty system, has the military-bureaucratic system built more common institutions or strengthened old ones? What are these institutions and how well do they stand up to the four criteria above? First, a major development, the creation of new states, will be discussed from the point of view of the problems of communal integration. Analysis will then proceed to the institutions built to integrate these states.

NATIONAL INTEGRATION

Problem of Communal Integration

Before 1967, Nigeria was made up of four regions: three in the south and one in the north. The northern region had more people than the three southern states combined (30 million to 26 million). In land area the northern region comprised more than three-fifths of Nigeria.[8]

Table 3.1
Population of Nigeria by Regions: Before April 1967

Region	Population	% of Total
North	29,809,000	55
East	12,394,000	21
West	10,931,000	20
Mid-West	2,536,000	4
Total	55,670,000	100

Table 3.2
Population of Nigeria after Division into States (April 1967)

State	Population
North Western	5,733,296
North Central	4,098,305
Kano	5,774,842
North Eastern	7,793,444
Benue Plateau	4,009,408
Kwara	2,399,365
Lagos	1,443,567
Western	9,487,525
Mid-Western	2,535,835
East-Central	6,223,831
South Eastern	4,626,317
Rivers	1,544,314

The unequal balance of populations and land areas of the various regions had several political consequences.

1. Political power was unevenly distributed as a result of the lopsided structure of the federation—that is, one region could rule the whole country for as long as it wished, even if its policies were not acceptable to everyone. What exacerbated this particular problem was that the political parties derived most (if not all) of their political support from the locally dominant ethnic group in the region in which the parties were based.

2. This meant that the minority ethnic groups in each region had to go along with whatever the major ethnic group did. The political party in each state sought to consolidate its power in an inherently unbalanced federal system; the fierce competition that ensued permitted no complaints from minority ethnic groups, who were often repressed.

3. The number of possible coalitions of political units was severely limited. The restriction on the number of possible coalitions was reinforced by the certainty that the north could always prevail. If one unit among several always had its way in a power game, the game certainly cannot last long, unless that single powerful unit is capable of satisfying the demands of all the others.[9] But since the demands were antithetical in the Nigerian situation— for instance the south was well ahead of the north developmentally, and, therefore, problems were often not coterminous—the possibility that the single powerful unit would be allowed to remain so was remote.

The southern regions had the alternative of forming a coalition against the north. The single, most dangerous potential threat to the stability of the Nigerian federal system during the 1960s was a north-south political confrontation. This ever-threatening possibility, an important factor in the civil war, was approached in a very obscure way by the political parties, since commissions were appointed but their recommendations never followed. Such an approach not only prevented any guarantee of the political rights of minority ethnic groups, but also ensured that no common organizations or institutions developed that might earn the trust of all or most of the political units. Therefore, no institutions capable of earning political legitimacy would be developed. The common political organizations that existed before 1960, the year of political independence from Britain—for instance the Common Services Board and the Federal Public Service Commission—were ridden with nepotism and corruption.

The issue thus became how to redraw the political map of Nigeria so that no one state or region could dominate the rest. One approach was to break up the existing four regions into many more regions or states, in which the main ethnic groups would have adequate representations and be able to feel that they could affect the outcomes of their own actions. This, it was assumed, would reduce certain groups' feelings of powerlessness and would ensure that national resources were shared equitably. Also, if states were created so that no one group could dominate the other, the character of competition would change. The number and variety of possible coalitions would increase, producing overlapping relationships among coalitions and, generally, more or less fluid patterns of cross-cutting associations of groups based on mutual interests and salience of demands.[10] The Efiks and Ibibios in the former Eastern region (secessionist Biafra) have continually complained that the Ibos have repressed them. (The Efiks and the Ibibios number about one-half of the total population of what was the Eastern region.) The demand for a new state resulted in agitations and riots before the military government acceded to power.

A similar situation arose in the West and in the North. In the West, the Edo, Itsekiri, and western Ibos agitated for their own state because, they complained, the Yorubas who controlled the dominant party in that region diverted all developmental projects to the Yoruba areas. This dominant party was the official opposition at the national level from 1954 to 1966, which left it in a vulnerable position, especially because of the obvious moves of the northern-based party which controlled the federal government to dismember the opposition. The federal opposition party was dismembered in 1962 and 1963; only then was a new region (the fourth) created by carving out the Midwest (Benin, Itsekiri, western Ibo) region. This gesture was actually designed to break the back of the opposition party. Agitation for a separate state by the Tiv, a minority ethnic group in the North, for a Middle Belt State, was repressed by the army and police. The dominant party on the national level supported the creation of a new state in the West, but opposed it in the North, the region from which it derived its power.

In short, the members of multiparty system did not seriously move to solve the minority problem, even though they believed that creating new states would reduce tensions. De Smith has observed that in Nigeria each regional government contrived to strengthen its own position at elections held after independence. It was possible to conjure up visions of an interregional entente, whereby each party in office would try to withdraw support from minority groups in other regions so that the federation would eventually comprise three or four loosely associated single party regimes with a coalition at the center.[11] Because one single party (and therefore one region) could destroy, manipulate, or enhance the interest of any other region as it deemed fit, there was no basis from which any meaningful coalition could emerge based on equal partnership. Wheare has argued that a viable federal system of government exists when, among other factors, each single regional authority is coordinated with and not subject to any of the others.[12] Since this was not the case in Nigeria, there was no basis for a strong federation.

Wheare is not absolutely correct, however, since there are other equally compelling reasons for the establishment of a workable federal system. Federalism becomes a necessity when there are very large areas to administer and where regional diversities are really important, as in Nigeria.[13] Furthermore, there are compelling economic reasons for the regions of Nigeria to associate together. The north is landlocked and needs coastal ports, there is complementarity in agricultural products (grains in the north and tree crops in the south), and there was a history of interregional trade before and during colonial rule. In general, the

Map 3.1
Regions of Nigeria — Before 1967

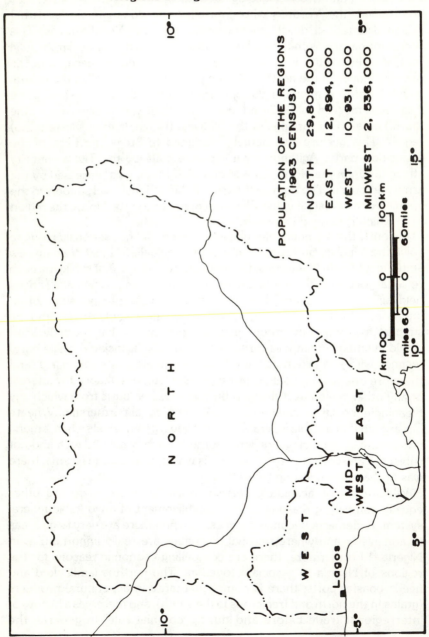

POPULATION OF THE REGIONS
(1963 CENSUS)

NORTH   29,809,000
EAST   12,894,000
WEST   10,951,000
MIDWEST 2,536,000

Map 3.2
States of Nigeria — After 1967

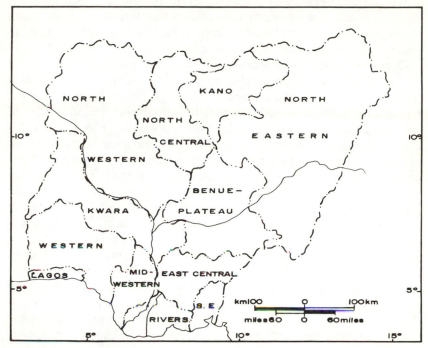

economic policies of a government are more effective when they are applied on a federation-side basis. For instance, social services would benefit from standardization of services and economies of scale,[14] from greater opportunity to support administrative specialization, from a more solid financial basis on which they might be supported, and from subsidies which might be given to poorer regions to help them meet minimum standards.[15] A final reason for a federalized Nigeria is that the country was previously administered by a single colonial authority; thus similar political institutions exist, which constitute an important basis of union.

The democratic, multiparty system failed to work vigorously to foster political stability. The argument could be raised, however, that the fault lay not in the democratic model, but in its faulty operation; that the newer democracies in the developing world may not have evolved a workable democratic model. Yet in some of the older democracies, minorities have been equally neglected. For instance, the attitude of Quebec toward the Jehovah's Witnesses and the Communists, and the attitude of Bavaria under the Weimar Republic towards Jews and Social Democrats, are cases in point. These may be extreme examples, but they do illustrate a generally negative orientation of majority groups towards minority groups. Majority communities have often exhibited a kind of xenophobic intolerance, which is accentuated when the minority belongs to a different ethnic group, believes in a different religion, or speaks a different language. Each of the Nigerian minorities is characterized by more than one of the criteria above. De Smith argued that it is more satisfying for the majority to appeal to democratic principles and impose their will.[16]

One might argue that federalism could easily shade off into separatism or further fragmentation of already poor and economically unviable regions. Indeed, in Nigeria, as in many parts of Africa, federalist sentiment based on creation of more states has poignant connotations of ethnocentrism. For example, there were sporadic public demands for more states, especially by a section of western and a few northern states. In Nigeria, members of a community which happens to be geographically concentrated in identifiable areas of a nation call for self-determination because they claim to have experienced inequitable treatment by the dominant majority. They want to be certain they receive fair shares of jobs in the public service, and equal opportunity to schools, scholarships, and funds for economic development. They feel that their religion and culture will be submerged unless they are given some measure of self-determination.[17]

Where agitation for more states is used as an obscurantist cover for separatism, it is an unacceptable form of pluralism. But when resistance to the creation of more states (as an extension of federalism) represents hostility to the minorities demanding it, the political system is actively courting political instability.

In effect, there are two antithetical pressures in the polity: the need to cater to the demands of minorities by ensuring the articulation and full expression of such demands through federalism; and the need for a strong central government (as the demand for a strong central government builds up pressure inimical to federalism). How did the military-bureaucratic system create the states or respond to the antithetical pressures noted above?

Mechanisms and Theoretical Implications

Increasingly, in Africa and the rest of the third world, authoritarian systems are being commended as being positively superior to western democratic models. Many social scientists have argued that the military-bureaucratic system appears to be, on the basis of its performance, a viable alternative to the multiparty democratic system.[18]

The argument has been frequently advanced that while liberal democracy, with its checks and balances, is an eminently desirable system of rule in appropriate circumstances, it may be a luxury in a situation where people are not sophisticated along western democratic lines. Many African nations, incuding Nigeria, had clearly moved in the direction of the one-party system even before the military took over, with many of them using highly repressive methods to govern. The manner in which one assesses such a system rests on the degree of authoritarianism and the policies actually pursued by the government in power. Thus, an important contribution to comparative political and sociological thought will be an assessment of the relative balance of coercion, persuasion, and compromise.

The Nigerian military government created twelve states by decree in May 1967 after consulting with political leaders and bureaucrats, and after reviewing previous recommendations and demands. This immediate creation of states underscores the direct action of the military style of politics, as opposed to the prevarication of the party system, in solving national problems. The military's directness, swiftness, and assured lack of opposition had an electrifying effect on operational efficiencies. It got things done and in sharp contrast to the party system style of leadership. After assuming office, the military government laid down nine guidelines of action, a cardinal principle being the investigation of minority problems and the creation of states. The military government's intention to correct previous imbalances was effectively carried out, thus fulfilling one of the objectives with which it assumed power. Another guideline which has direct bearing on the creation of states is a new population census which is being currently carried out. This step was acclaimed by most Nigerian citizens.

Many politicians who lost power during the creation of states were co-opted into the governments of the new states, if they had not been previously found guilty by tribunals of corruption. Those citizens or groups who had complaints about boundaries, or who wanted more states created, were requested to wait until the post-civil-war reconstruction and rehabilitation was completed, as planned for in the national development plan. Those who continued to agitate after this plea were threatened with the use of force. This procedure again contrasts with what took place during the democratic multiparty regime when the Tiv ethnic group in northern Nigeria agitated for self-determination between 1960 and 1964. The long-drawn rebellion was repressed by the armed forces, and negotiations were not initiated by the party in control. As the figures given below indicate, several hundred people were killed without any concrete steps taken to allay the group's fears.

The Nigerian military often takes initial steps to satisfy demands, persuades or compromises if further demands arise, and issues threats to regulate such demands if it has no means to meet them, or if it considers them obscurantist. Elaborating on the steps taken toward persuasion, the military has sought to approach the dissenters by going through the chiefs. In the western states of Nigeria in 1970 and 1971, agitation arose for the breakup of the state into two. The federal and western state military governments invited some high-ranking bureaucrats along with traditional chiefs to discuss the problems. The roles now being reasserted at the local level by the traditional chiefs were performed by party officials during the multiparty regime. This patrimonial tendency in military rulerships resembles the colonial framework of authority, where the alliance of governor, bureaucrats, and chiefs was familiar. A political system which ignores the influence of traditional chiefs is hardly likely to reach down to the grass roots, however democratic it is supposed to be. Indeed, the relationships between the political structure and the demands made upon it to solve tasks are crucial in understanding political stability.

INSTITUTIONS AND DEVELOPMENT OF POLITICAL AND NATIONAL INTEGRATION

The creation of states cannot by itself guarantee political development and stability; it can even encourage separatism unless governmental cooperation is established through integrating institutions.

What new institutions have been built and how have the old ones been reinforced? By what mechanisms are these new institutions fostering national integration?

Administrative Institutions

The federal military government established by decree national councils for specific subjects areas (such as personnel and establishment, education, housing, agriculture, finance, works, health). These councils serve as consultative bodies for national coordination of activities. Each council operates at two levels: at the permanent secretary's level and at the civilian commissioner's level. Meetings are held twice a year in rotation among the state capitals, and different council meetings are in session simultaneously in different parts of the country. There is an air of constant and virile activity at the intergovernmental level throughout the year. Representatives of each state government report back directly to their military government. This reporting channel is worthy of note since recommendations are binding on each state government.

The institutional structure of this cooperative machinery is not limited to form councils. Consultations are continued between official meetings, and this is where interpersonal relationships among the military governors become important. Due to relationships developed in the military circles, military governors have established communication among themselves. Military governors discuss special requests or problems between themselves in an informal way, while state officials carry through with the suggestions.

Such informal communication among military governors is not unique; all top administrators engage in this type of communication. Watts argued that when financial or administrative responsibility for particular matters rests with one government or another, but where the interests of both governments will be affected by the decisions taken, consultation through formal and informal devices may be required in order to communicate to the other government the values and objectives involved before it acts.[19] One such important area is the training and transfer of personnel. Effective formal and informal communication has been developed between many southern states and some northern states. These southern states sent in engineers, education officers, and teachers to help these newer states stand on their feet.[20] In general, because the states, as political actors, perceive the National Council on Personnel and Establishment as a decision-making center that will satisfy their demands, they tend to address their demands to this new center. Since this is the only administrative-political institution through which personnel demands can be satisfied, and since the institution has been appreciably successful in reaching decisions favored by the states, the states are beginning to expect that future decisions will be rewarding too. More and more demands are being made. Southern states are inundated with requests from other states for trained personnel.[21] The effectiveness of these councils has gradually ensured the legitimacy of these institutions, quite apart from the fact that they were legitimately created by government.

The Western state (whose capital is the same as the old Western region and which therefore had the personnel of the old region) is one major supplier to the newer states. Although this state was ready to help other states, there were shortages in crucial areas.[22] In response to this, the federal military government created a service pool into which top administrators are put and called up for the states when needed. This operates as an extension of the National Council on Personnel and Establishment. Since new demands are constantly being made and additional decision making required, further integration and the extension of the institution's field of action will be required.

The character of the demands that are emerging is such that this spillover effect is increasing. Whether by design or otherwise, this spillover mechanism is being used to arrive at decisions which will have consequences outside of their original area of power. The National Council on Agriculture makes decisions that will predictably influence decisions in the National Council on Personnel and Establishments. If this were done by design, then it could be argued that the institutions were seeking to stimulate the emergence of growth-inducing supporting coalitions, which require decisions that can only be made by expanding the task of the institutions. The process of integration thus acquires its own dynamism; that is, if properly used, institutions have the character of a process of self-sustained growth.[23]

The creation of the new service pool affected the other councils' decisions, since qualified personnel remained a scarce resource. For instance, decisions affecting the establishment of a joint agricultural project between two northern states, a matter clearly under the jurisdiction of the National Council on Agriculture, had to await decisions of the personnel council. The two councils developed informal administrative contacts in order to link up with each other. In general, when a decision requires additional decisions in other areas for its implementation, new linkages among new institutions are established. Such new linkages make for integration at the intergovernmental level. If the states' boundaries are more or less coterminous with ethnic or communal geographical boundaries, the argument could be made that ethnic groups (or at least their leaders) believe their interests are served by this new institution.

In several of these councils, nongovernmental actors have become involved. For instance the indigenization policy of the federal military government, by which foreign firms have been authorized to increase the percentage of their Nigerian indigenous staff, and by which certain of these firms have to sell majority holdings of their shares to Nigerian indigenes, requires structural transformations in the business-education field and also in the administration of business finances. Reports to be made to the military government by the National Councils on Education and Finance would require information dealing with the progress of this indigenization policy. Since many of the foreign corporations perceive active participation by Nigerians in their business as an insurance against outright nationalization of such businesses, they have been willing to cooperate with institutions of government in training indigenous citizens[24] and in changing their financial policies. For example, the Bank of West Africa and Barclays Bank (a subsidiary of Chase Manhattan) have altered their lending practices to suit new demands.[25] Also, these councils are receiving support from other nongovernmental bodies such as chambers of commerce. Since these institutions have succeeded in acquiring the support of important nongovernmental actors in the various Nigerian states, it becomes more likely that those state governments will support policies that favor such institutions. In turn, the activities and decisions of these institutions as related above are believed to attract cooperation

from increasing and increasingly significant coalitions of state governments. All of this strengthens the legitimacy of the institutions. These
institutions now manipulate and consciously employ mechanisms of
coalition from among the various state units, whether they are
governmental or not.

In effect, Nigeria has not only had many more governmental units as
actors, it has had more nongovernmental actors such as commercial
firms. There were only four regional governments during the regime of the
multiparty system, and the struggle for political power among the parties
prevented interregional cooperation on such a scale as now exists.
Although the multiparty regime had some consultative bodies, political
and administrative forces weakened their appeal.[26] Before 1966, such
bodies as the National Economic Council and the Joint Planning
Committee existed. Yet the councils' decisions had no binding force on
the regions. Indeed, the 1962-66 economic development plan was a
conglomerate of the plans of these separately powerful regions. The Joint
Planning Committee could not coordinate anything. Today the plan is
more integrated since each state has to submit its plan long in advance of
committee meetings, and experts must work to integrate them. Again, a
National Council on Establishment had existed, but all of the regions had
laws which definitely precluded any interstate movement of personnel.
The federal military has breathed life into the old councils and established
many new councils. Before 1966, if a particularly powerful region, such as
the North, did not favor a policy, it had enough political power to
manipulate and defeat it at the federal level. But today, since there are
twelve instead of four regions, the relative significance of the support of
each political unit for these institutions is diminished. What has resulted
are new coalitions of political actors.[27]

The Benue-Plateau or Kwara state (both parts of the former northern
region) have entered into governmental agreements, such as personnel
exchange, with the Midwest state, a southern state. This situation breaks
the threat of a north-south coalition, which was instrumental in destroying
the first republic. As Deutsch argued, concrete steps toward integration
will be taken on the basis of varying coalitions of supporting groups. While
such coalitions need not necessarily rest upon complete identity of
demands, Deutsch further argued that they display some measure of
complementarity, since the states must see some integrative step as
conducive to the realization of whatever demands they may otherwise
have.[28] The interlocking, overlapping demands among southern states
and among groups of states across old north-south frontier lines have
created a political situation characterized by divisions that cut deeply
across the old political units and regions. Since the divisions are becoming
more varied and more salient, the new cross-cutting divisions support the

legitimacy of the new nation. The common institutions that have been established have created interest coalitions and cross-cutting divisions from pluralistic political communities.[29] These coalitions are significantly modifying the political system and are generating mechanisms that tend to lead to a self-sustained process of integration.

The type of interstate cooperation described above might eventually become a way of resisting increased centralization and preserving federalism. States may now prefer to act cooperatively when they cannot act alone, rather than let the federal government take the initiative.[30] During the multiparty regime, however, states started out unusually strong. The federal government took the initiative in an increasing number of decision-making areas because the states chose to act alone and, in this way, became progressively weaker.

Strengthening of Old Administrative Institutions

Deutsch claimed that integrative capabilities are closely related to the general ability of a given political unit to act. If administrative systems are advanced and expanded, they become cores of strength around which integrative processes develop.[31] In this section, we will examine the impact of the integrative mechanism described above on the administrative system of the states and on the expansion of the federal administrative system.

The government of the Western state has coordinated its relations with other states under the military governor's office.[32] Further investigation of the channels used to coordinate intergovernmental activities elsewhere revealed that the trend was similar to the practice adopted by the West. Each government tended to coordinate its relationship with other state governments through a governmental department. For example, in Australia, the Premier's conference is the preeminent senior government body, and consequently, the prime minister's or premier's office has taken on the major role of coordinating state activities with other states.[33] Since it is important not to permit the different ministries of a state government to duplicate demands or relationships with other states or to work at cross-purposes with each other, the trend toward cooperation has facilitated coordination of the varied and complex patterns of intergovernmental administrative relationships which have developed in Nigeria. In the multiparty days, experts tended to work out isolated, piecemeal relationships; now the experts must be cleared by the military governor's office, which coordinates intergovernmental activities, so the character of intergovernmental bargaining and accommodation has changed.

In general, this tendency to reduce interstate (interethnic) conflicts to the decisions of administrative experts has meant increased bureaucratization, which in turn has made cooperation easier by taking these problems out of the arena of politics. A crucial issue is whether this generates a tendency for problem areas in general to be subsumed under intergovernmental coordination, making it more difficult to reach agreement because issues are political and not just technical. The answer to this question lies in the two-tier setup of intergovernmental cooperation. Besides meetings by administrative officials, state commissioners meet regularly to discuss political aspects of issues, but they transfer only the more technical aspects to the administrators. The Rivers people belong to a different ethnic group from the Ibos of East Central state, and each governmental area of jurisdiction coincides with ethnic boundaries. An interstate conflict developed between the Rivers and East Central states over the return of Ibo property in Portharcourt, the current Rivers state capital, but formerly an important coastal port of the Eastern region (former Biafra). The Rivers people were opposed to the secession of Biafra. They were instrumental in helping federal Nigerian forces gain a foothold in the secessionist territory. After the collapse of the Biafran forces, the Rivers state emerged as a separate government. However, Portharcourt was predominantly occupied by Ibos, who still owned most of the property. If all Ibo property was returned, Portharcourt, capital of Rivers state, would virtually revert to Ibo control. Yet the federal government insisted that all Ibo property be returned. The political issue of who will control the city has to be resolved; in part, this is related to agreements worked out by experts as to the feasibility of selling some of the properties to Rivers people. Even though this conflict has not been completely resolved, the machinery now exists to work out an accommodation.

More recently, the governor of the East Central state has said that he believes the most viable solution to this problem lies along the path of dialogue based on honor, mutual understanding, and fidelity.[34] Broad political agreements may well be worked out at the civilian commissioners' meetings, while the bureaucrats work out the details concerning documentary evidence of property ownership.[35]

Effectiveness of Central Administration System

The broader task of coordinating national activities rests with the federal administration. As Watts argued, unless an effective and efficient central administration is involved in intergovernmental activities, the institutional machinery for cooperation is unlikely to be effective.[36] To what extent has the scope of the federal administrative system been expanded, relative to the regime of the multiparty system? This question will be answered at two conceptual levels: (1) the shift in the focus of decision-making power from politicians to bureaucrats; and (2) the structural differentiation that derives from the expanded capacity to cope with purely organizational tasks at the federal administrative level. The growth of governmental institutions is an important clue to its structural development. Due to the bureaucratic orientation of the military, the rate of expansion now is greater than it was in the years immediately preceding the military takeover of government.

Bureaucrats and Politicians. The struggle between the bureaucrats and the politicians in developing nations has been well-documented. There are important differences in background training: the bureaucrats generally have more education than the politicians; bureaucrats have a more conservative outlook emphasizing more gradual development, in contrast to politicians who want faster progress. Yet there is a close affinity in background training and orientation between the bureaucrats and the military. Though the military has allegedly intervened to mediate the conflict between politicians and bureaucrats, in practice the military has depended on the bureaucrats for expert decision making. Bureaucracy accords well with the military organizational characteristics of precision, order, and coordination.

In post-civil-war Nigeria, bureaucrats have tended to acquire power at the expense of civilian commissioners. The power of civilian commissioners as politicians in the present government is much more restricted than in prewar days. For instance, the bureaucrats, because the military depends on them, have greater capacity to initiate policies (especially if they can draw up policies which will win the favor of the military), in the area of national reconstruction and rehabilitation (such as resettlement schemes of displaced persons, rehabilitation of ousted government officials and injured military personnel, and so on). Civil servants now feel less restricted from decision making than during the regime of the politicians. This view was echoed by governmental officials in other states — West, East Central, and Midwest — three of the four regional governments from before the civil war.

The military often leaves large areas of decision-making power not clearly defined. This is a concomitant development of its dependence on the bureaucracy. For instance, military-bureaucratic efficiency sometimes requires direct contact and reports from bureaucrats to military officials in government. Many top bureaucrats in the federal service are chairmen of new national councils and members of other new governmental agencies. They report directly to the cabinet or the office of the military head of state, and not to any particular civilian commissioner. The civilian commissioner who structurally is in the intervening position may thus be bypassed. While this is by no means the legal structure, a perception of such shifts in their favor encourages bureaucrats to move into and consolidate such new power roles. That is, the tendency is stronger to systematically undermine the power position of the civilian politicians. In the structure of decision making — which involves the civilian commissioners, the bureaucrats, and the military — the civilian commissioners appear to wield the least power.

It could be argued that the operational efficiency generated by removing issues from the political arena helps the nation develop rapidly. That is, the attenuation of the power of the politician reduces prevarication and ambivalence and encourages movement into direct policy execution (see Figure 3.1).

Figure 3.1
Structural Changes in the Organization of the Nigerian Government Ministry

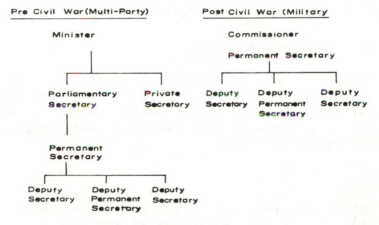

Figure 3.1 shows that the positions of parliamentary and private secretaries (both political appointments) have been eliminated, thus permitting direct access to civilian commissioners. In the pre-civil-war period, the parliamentary and private secretaries were so powerful that they often got in the way of direct communication between the minister (a politician) and the permanent secretary (a bureaucrat). The bureaucrats have tended to reassert the powers they had in the colonial period because the military government now emphasizes to the commissioners that they (commissioners) were appointed and not elected. This awareness reduces the extent to which commissioners can behave like former politicians.

While the bureaucrats have become stronger, problems may develop if and when civilian politicians return to power.

Structural Differentiation in Federal Public Office. Structural reorganization has taken place, as a consequence of the need to widen the scope of government activity, by broadening areas in which government is involved, such as education, social welfare, health services, and so forth. The government has also assumed increased responsibility for enhancing economic development and planning, collecting data, and training and hiring new staff. The military government has fashioned new instruments to handle these new concerns. Prime examples are in the Ministry of Economic Planning and the Federal Office of Statistics.

Since 1967, the Ministry of Economic Planning has added several new divisions to take care of the coordination of national councils set up. Such new divisions include the economic coordination unit and rehabilitation units. In addition, the Federal Office of Statistics, which had once handled census matters, no longer does so. Presently, there is a new Department of Census. The increased pace of activity has opened up improved communication among the various governmental departments, which attests to the bureaucratic coordination of the military.

Personnel Expansion of Government

The new divisions, which involve the recruitment of new staff (see Table 3.3), additional higher responsibilities assumed by older staff, and new interdepartmental linkages together result in increased role and structural differentiation in the administration. Table 3.3 shows the rapid increase in staff between 1964 and 1971.

Table 3.3
Nigeria — Employment of High-Level Manpower by Type of Employer, 1964 and 1971

Federal and Regional 1964/1971 state goverments	Local govern- ments	Public Boards	Private Establish- ment	Total
1964 27,401	10,192	4,344	15,956	57,893
1971* 41,500	12,000	6,400	25,000	78,900

Sources : Nigeria High-Level Manpower Study, No. 2. Federal printer, Lagos, 1964, Federal and State Gazettes 1969-71 ; Handbook of Nigeria, 1970, 1971, Lagos Nigeria.
*The 1971 figures are not very reliable since they depended on estimation.

Table 3.3 reveals that in 1964 the government was the largest employer of high-level manpower (47%). This relative percentage had not changed much in 1971, but the interesting fact is that the number of people employed by government had increased by over 50%, indicating the addition of a great number of new staff to man the new divisions and new state governments. The table shows that government employment per 1,000 of population rose from 0.5 to 0.74, a measure of expansion. The total number of high-level manpower also jumped by more than 33%. This is a remarkable achievement, in view of the fact that the nation had just emerged from a war. But how has the military government trained this new staff? Between 1963 and 1968, 17,822 Nigerians were in various educational institutions in Nigeria and abroad. In 1972, the figure had more than doubled to slightly below 36,000. The military government had embarked upon a crash program to expand the universities and raise the Nigerian universities output by 100% before 1974.

In his budget speech on April 1, 1973, General Gowon said: "The federal government is ever conscious of the fact that the successful achievement of its economic and social objectives depends to a very large extent on an efficient and well-organized government machinery as well as on well-trained, conscientious and disciplined personnel at all levels of its undertakings. It will therefore continue with its program of intensive and extensive training of staff at all levels."[37] A decree was subsequently promulgated to establish the Administrative Staff College of Nigeria for top administrators in both public and private sectors.[38]

Table 3.4
Nigerian Educational Enrollments (in thousands)

	1964	1965	1966	1967 *	1968**	1969/70
Primary	2849	2911	3026	3000	3000	5200
Secondary	205.0	208.7	211.3	190	195	281.2
University	6.7	7.7	8.9	7.1	8.6	9.7

*does not include figures for East Central state.
Sources: Economic Commission for Africa - Summaries of Economic data. Paper, 071-752. U.S.A.T.D. (PPC/SRD Revision no. 236)

Educational Expansion

The figures in Table 3.4 reveal gradual educational expansion from 1967 onward, with phenomenal increases registered in 1969 and 1970. (The 1967 and 1968 figures reflect the effect of war at all levels.) The federal military government established several federal secondary schools to promote a nationally-oriented high school system. Such schools would admit students from all over the federation to enhance national unity. The 1970-74 development plan aimed at achieving a national minimum enrollment of 50% at the primary-school level and 25% at the secondary-school level. Even though the government is still far from the target (current enrollment figures are 30% at the primary school and 15% at the secondary school level), the figures are substantially higher than what the multiparty system achieved in six years. The military government has achieved this by special crash projects in education, particularly for the poorer areas. These developments have been responsible for expansion in staff and expenditure, as shown in Table 3.5.

Table 3.5
Expenditure — Federal Ministry of Education

	Actual Expenditure 1970/71	Estimate 1972/73	Approved Estimate 1971/72	Increase
Personal Enrollment (Staff salaries)	502,205	1,128,960	800,420	328,540
Other changes	1,066,025	2,699,880	1,412,820	1,287,067
Special Expenditure	33,243	147,810	255,280	-107,470
Total	1,601,473	3,976,650	2,468,520	-107,470
Net Increase		1,508,130		

Source: Federal Republic of Nigeria Approved Recurrent Estimates. Federal Ministry of Information, Lagos, Nigeria, 1972.

The above table reveals that federal goverment expenditure (approved estimates 1972/73) is more than twice the amount spent in 1970/71 and twice the amount spent in any year before 1966. The expansion in expenditure reflect the expanded activities and structural differentiation of government administration.

Federal government expenditures (approved estimates 1972-73) are more than twice the amount spent in any year before 1966. The increased expenditures reflect the expanded activities and structural differentiation of government administration.

Transportation

Similar expansion occurred in the transport system (rail and road) both of which have been under governmental general administration (although special agencies were established to manage them). Figures of completed roads do not reflect the complexity of activities now going on. For instance, road systems increased from 55,256 in 1966 to nearly 60,000 in 1971. But work in several parts of the country is proceeding on road projects totalling over 5,000 miles. In his budget speech of April 1973, General Gowon announced that construction had been completed on 855 miles of tarred road. Another 4,625 miles of road were scheduled to be completed before December 1973.[39]

Military Manpower

The chapter on methodology indicated that a substantial military establishment leads to an elaborate and distinctly modern political structure. Nigerian military manpower rose from 8,000 men in the pre-1966 period to its current total of 250,000; that is, from 0.14 per 1,000 population to 4.2 per 1,000 population. This represents a substantial increase which has spillover effects into other areas of governmental activity, such as training of personnel, provision of social services, and so on. Table 3.6 illustrates changes in defense expenditure which reflect the massive increase in military expansion.

Table 3.6
Federal Government Defense Expenditure — Million Nigerian Pounds Convert at 1:2.8 U.S. Dollars

Multi-party regime				Military regime				
1963	1964	1965	1967	1968	1969	1970	1971	1972/73*
		53.4	81.4	180.0	157.4	107.2	120.1	

*Approved Estimates
Sources :   Recurrent estimates of the government of the Federal Republic of Nigeria, 1963-1973. Central Bank of Nigeria Annual Survey Reports, 1963-1973. U.S.A.I.D. Summary of Basic Data on Nigeria, July, 1972.

Table 3.6 indicates that military expenditure rose by more than 1,000 percent from 1963 to 1973. Even though the civil war ended in 1967, defense expenditure did not decrease by an appreciable amount in the three years after the war. The government wanted to maintain the relatively elaborate framework of military organization. Today, the Nigerian military is the largest and most modern in sub-Saharan Africa, with the possible exception of South Africa. Besides the new Air Force and Navy, other new divisions include an engineering corps and a signal corps comparable to that described by Pye in reference to the Burmese military.[40]

The federal military government has made constitutional break-throughs and built or strengthened institutions which have had far more positive effects on communal integration than the party system did. What are the direct empirical results of their achievements? Despite these advances, do communal conflicts remain at the level that existed during the multiparty regime? Table 3.7 reveals that communal conflicts have shown an overall decrease, relative to those that occurred during the multiparty regime.

Table 3.7
Communal Instability in Nigeria: 1963-1965, 1970-1973

Event, Date and Type of government	Characteristics
1. Rebellion August-October 1960, 1964 multi-party system	(a) Description : (In mid-1960, groups of Tiv (50-150 strong) burned the houses of chiefs and politicians and about 25 people were killed). Rebellion was renewed in February 1964 and the Nigerian army engaged in a counter attack for the rest of 1964. Estimates of those killed ranged from 1000 to 3000.
	(b) Apparent Causes: Tiv elevants demanded greater autonomy in the northern region.
2. Riot and Rebellion September 1965 to Jan. 1966 Multi-party system	(a) Description: In Western Nigeria, political party conflicts resulted in severe acts of violence in which several hundred people were murdered in open daylight on public streets or in their homes. Estimates of those killed ranged from 500 to 1000.
	(b) Apparent Causes: Dissatisfaction wity party-in-power's handling of the 1965 election. Hostility was also directed to elements of the Hausa-Fulani group which gave support to that party.

Civil war, May 1967 – January 1970, took place and both were under military rule. We omitted the period 1966 - 1970 from active consideration because this was a period when the country was essentially unsettled and nobody knew whether Nigeria would be one or not. Secondly, the complete breakdown of law and order occurred during the regime of the party system. Thirdly, data collected during a war are not typical of a more peaceful period and in any case we have restricted active consideration to specific periods (as above).

Sources: John p. Macintosh et al (eds) Nigeria Government and Politics (Evanston III Northwestern University Press, 1966) pp. 498-501. Africa Report Series 1961-73; West Africa 1970-73.

As noted earlier, the chief source of communal instability has been the denial of minority rights—a situation taken care of by the creation of states. The data show that there have been no communal conflicts since the end of the civil war between Biafra (spearheaded by Ibos) and the rest of the Nigerian Federation. The states are now concerned with consolidating internal resources as well as external relations with other states. One could argue that a conflict could not be expected so shortly after a bloody civil war, and that the war is a tacit deterrent against further communal riots. However, groups which were agitating for more states only suspended further action when the federal military government promised to examine their grievances after the current development period and had set in motion machinery, such as a census, that would help determine the real character of such needs. Perhaps the military tactics induced acquiescence, not the fact that the groups were tired from fighting a war.

We have emphasized bureaucratic coordination and order, both military organizational characteristics, in the setting up of national councils, and in the programs for interstate flow of communication and personnel. Of course, the military-bureaucratic model will not work for all time, although it is effective now. The military is laying the basis for communal integration, but in the long run, the ability of this model to contain tension may be strained.

Bureaucratic and political institutions are not only performing symbolic governmental functions. They also perform instrumental functions, as well as expressive functions, for the general population. That is, they create and also sustain an impression which induces acquiescence by the general public in the face of a political situation which might produce resentment, resistance, and instability.

Administrative institutions in which Ibos, Yorubas, Hausas, Binis, Kanuris, and others operate together effectively become an alliance of openly hostile and rival ethnic groups. Such institutions serve as organizationally and psychologically effective aspects of the political system. At the same time, they help to provide a predictable and stable setting within which the organized ethnic groups concerned use their weapons with minimal anxiety. As public agencies, these institutions evoke and manipulate the myths, rituals, and other symbols of the state. Edelman argues that the creation of such administrative and political institutions in a policy area may signal the emergence of a changed relationship between groups labeled as adversaries.[41] The creation of states and the establishment of coordinating administrative institutions constitute the assurance that neither the Yorubas, the Hausas, the Ibos, the Binis or the Efiks can push any bargaining advantage to the point of eliminating the others. The limited competition allowed to these groups in the framework described permits free expression of dissent, cooperation, and a healthy sense of rivalry, in contrast to the cut-throat competition that characterized the party regime.

ELITE-MASS INCOME DIFFERENTIAL AND RURAL-URBAN DEVELOPMENT GAP

As discussed in Chapter 1, the gap in income between the small elite and the large masses of the people is a very real weakness in the polity, since it has been responsible for riots, protest demonstrations, and industrial unrest. Most of the better paid workers obtain employment in the cities, such as in government agencies or industry; most of the others, who work as peasants in the countryside, have little annual income and are, therefore, motivated to migrate to the cities in search of better employment. The urban migration has been described as one of tropical Africa's worst problems because it gives rise to a large unemployed urban proletariat that is a potential source of political unrest. This group had a part in the political unrests which undermined law and order in 1965.

This large group of unemployed is often joined by salaried workers who are discontented with their pay. The problem, therefore, lies at the two levels indicated in the title: the gap in real income, and the gap in the rural-urban areas with consequent city-ward migration and unemployment. What are the likely solutions? What have the two political systems under consideration done, and with what results? A list follows: (1) revision of national income structure to reduce the gap; (2) generation of increased employment through the expansion of industry and the dispersion of such industries; (3) the improvement of agriculture.

Revision of National Income Structure

Between 1962 and 1966, the party system in power was forced to yield to the pressure of industrial unrest to revise the income structure. The guidelines for the Morgan Commission, set up at that time, were, broadly, to examine the income of the workers with a view to raising it. It did not contain any policy guidelines that could be built into a national income distribution policy. Created on an ad hoc basis, the recommendations and their subsequent implementation simply did nothing to reduce the gap. The military declared, as one of its aims, the reduction of this income gap. In 1970, it set up a Wage and Salary Review Commission whose aim, among others, was to examine the structure of income distribution.

A layout of the different policy guidelines under the two different regimes is found in Table 3.8. The guidelines stipulated by the party system restricted investigation and recommendations only to the public services, which reinforced the notion that the government was the chief source of income, and thus, tacitly encouraged movement to the cities, the seat of governmental activities. In contrast, policy guidelines under the military-bureaucratic system not only stipulated examination of the public services, but also of the private sectors. It also stipulated the need to harmonize income from both sectors. It examined the structure of income in the public and private sectors, while the guidelines for the earlier review was to examine income distribution within the framework of the existing differential wage structure in use by the governments. The restriction perpetuated, even increased, the gap in the income structure. Thus, the ratio of the top salary (in the public service) to the lowest, by 1966, was more than 28:1 (one of the highest in the world).

Table 3.8
Nigerian Policy Guidelines for Income Revision

Party System 1965	Military -Bureaucratic System 1970
1 To review the basic rates of salary at present payable by the government of the federation public services. 2. To review the rates of wages at present payable by the governments of the federation to daily rated workers within the framework of the differential wage structure at present in use by the government.	The Adebo Commission was charged with making recommendation in the light of (a) the cost of living and renumeration in posts with comparable responsibilities in the private sector (b) the requirement for the rapid development of the national economy (c) the adequate development and deployment of efficient manpower in the public service and other factors. I. To examine areas in which rationalization and harmonization of wages salaries and other income and conditions of employment are desirable and feasible as between the public and private sectors of the national economy. II. To consider the need to establish a system for ensuring that renumeration in the public services, the statutory public corporations and the state owned companies is periodically reviewed and kept in proper national balance. III. To examine the position of the rural population of Nigeria which indeed comprises the great majority of the country's inhabitants. IV. To examine the position of self employed persons, including professional men and women artisans. e.t.c. V. To examine the need to ensure maximum possible employment throughout the country. VI. To make recommendations which will ensure the importance of increased productivity both in the national interest and for ensuring a steady rise in the workers living standards.

Sources: Federal Republic of Nigeria - Review of Salaries and Wages Commission, Lagos, Federal Ministry of Information, 1967; Federal Republic of Nigeria, Report of the Wages and Salaries Review Commission - Federal Ministry of Information, Lagos Nigeria 1970.

In 1970, the Adebo Commission recommended a 40% wage increase for the lowest paid category, but did not recommend anything for the superscale, uppermost wage group. This immediately reduced pay differentials between highest and lowest paid from 28:1 to 16:1, an achievement of which the party system appeared incapable. The military government coped with resentment of this new development by promising to review wages again, but not before a two-year waiting period had elapsed; no general increase in the salaries and wages of all workers in the public services, corporations, or quasi-government companies was to be made for another 24 months. This decision contained an element of coercion in that it was final, but at the same time, the waiting period carried a tacit implication of anticipation which was enough to persuade dissenters to wait.

The federal government also accepted the commission's recommendations to curb inflation to reduce the cost of living for the lower paid groups, and to increase wages. These recommendations include the following.

1. Price controls on commodities (like food items) most commonly consumed by the low-income group. In the 1970 budget speech, the head of state emphasized that special efforts should be made to ensure that commodities consumed by people within the lower income group were not touched by import restrictions included in the budget for that year.

2. The establishment of a bulk-purchasing body to buy specific and most needed items in large quantities and sell them at subsidized prices to the low-income group. Efforts in this direction included commandeering the products of some local factories which produced essential commodities and effectively distributing such products. Even though the Price Control Board failed at first, due to poor data-gathering techniques, it did achieve a substantial reduction in commodity prices.

3. A rent control board to set rents and listen to complaints was set up.

4. A transportation board was established which recommended the following (which were accepted): (a) that the transportation board coordinate rate charges of commuters; (b) that fares in Lagos be streamlined so that passengers may pay one fare for a reasonable length of journey, even if they have to change buses; (c) that season tickets be issued at special rates for workers who use the buses regularly; (d) that each government accept the responsibility to regulate and coordinate public transport and review fares at regular intervals within its area of jurisdiction; (e) that restrictions be eased on the importation of those categories of vehicles and their spare parts which are essential for public transportation within urban areas.

The above recommendations have achieved substantial improvements for the workers and have created favorable perceptions of the present military government, as opposed to the party system which achieved comparatively less.

Industrial Expansion and Dispersal

Upon accession to power, the military government declared one of its objectives to be the reduction of unemployment through the encouragement of industry. The index of manufacturing production rose in 1970 by 18% to 250 (1963—100). The rise of 150% during the year the war ended signifies greater development, mobilization, and orientation toward expansion than during the regime of the parties. The number of people engaged in industry in 1972 was about 150% of those engaged in the comparative period before the war. Unemployment is still high due to the increase in the labor force and the displacement of large numbers of the working population by the war.

More significant for rural development is the declared aim of dispersing industries into the countryside. The Federal Commission for Industries reiterated that the government would disperse industries throughout the country as a matter of policy to ensure equitable development.[42] In pursuance of the objective, the federal government (1) established development centers for small scale, dispersed industries coordinated by local regional centers; (2) decided to reduce by one-half the concentration of industries in the capital city and stated that nine out of every ten new industries must be located outside of the Lagos areas.

Urban migration has brought tremendous pressure onto the cities. In his 1972-73 budget speech, the military governor of Lagos state (Lagos is the capital city of Nigeria), complained that pressure on basic services was increasing at an alarming rate, with more than 70% of the budget spent on social services, such as water, roads, health, and education.[43] In response to these pressures, the federal government announced a policy of subsidizing the states to supply water to rural areas. Thus, the North-Central state has been able to start construction of five big dams and the West state has undertaken the construction of 54 water supply schemes to the rural areas.

The federal government has also proceeded vigorously with the construction of road networks to open up the countryside and has started the construction of 18 new airports, which will not only link the new states but also open up the countryside. The specific aim is to establish regional centers to serve as points of coordination for the dispersal of industries into the countryside. With increased expansion, new centers will emerge around old centers.

Another significant development in this area is the setting up of 26 centers in rural areas throughout the federation to monitor, register, and locate the unemployed in all parts of the country. Announced in the head of state's budget speech of April 1973, this measure is also designed to encourage interstate movement of peoples, to inculcate a sense of unity and national purpose, and to reduce pressure on utilities in a few urban centers. However, one of the most significant steps taken to induce farmers and employment seekers to stay in the rural areas has been the review of the policy of payment to farmers through the marketing board.

Improvement of Agriculture: Marketing Boards and Farmers' Incomes

Policies concerned with the improvement of agriculture, in general, will be considered in Chapter 4. Here we shall focus narrowly on a specific policy that relates agriculture to farmers' incomes. The party system inherited the marketing board structure from the colonial government, which established it after World War II. The primary purpose of the marketing board was to ensure that the average price paid in Nigeria for export crops was substantially close to the average net price realized on the world markets, and that the board's buying and selling would approximately balance. All the marketing boards in the four commonwealth countries (Nigeria, Ghana, Sierra Leone, and Gambia) accumulated great surpluses. The surplus of more than 86 million pounds sterling (or $192 million) handed over to the government of Western Nigeria at the beginning of self-rule came from the marketing of cocoa (the main export crop of that region).

But how did the politicans use the marketing boards and with what consequences? The surpluses were only in part used to subsidize prices paid to farmers. They were largely diverted for party purposes. The marketing board became a major source of corruption in Nigeria, a powerful temptation to politicians. Some of the surpluses were used by the government to subsidize other sectors of the economy and, thereby, became a means of taxing farmers without admitting it. Sometimes, the party in power sought popularity by overpaying the farmers, especially around election times.

But farmers cannot be forced to play a role if they perceive that they are not getting a fair deal. Production of some crops has stagnated (for instance, cocoa), while production of other crops, like oil palm, has sharply declined. So much is raised from produce tax that it becomes a disincentive to farmers. The first report issued on the progress of the 1970-74 development plan stated that the marketing board system discouraged increased efforts and production by the farmers, and attributed stagnation in output and export of some cash crops to that system.[44] Thus, the Nigerian marketing board system made the farmers pay millions of pounds over and above their regular taxes, in sharp contrast with the practice in Western Europe, Canada, and the United States, where farmers have been subsidized.

Farmers have increased production of locally-produced crops, to the detriment of export crops, and have smuggled Nigerian cocoa and groundnut into the neighboring state of Dahomey. Farmers were underpaid not only in relation to other sectors of the Nigerian income groups, but also in relation to farmers in neighboring countries. Smuggling thus became inevitable when there were significant differences in prices paid to farmers between one country and another, and also between states within Nigeria. In consequence, Nigerian farmers showed violent resentment between 1964 and 1968.

What did the federal military government do to change the situation? In 1969, it appointed the Ayoola Commission to examine the causes of farmer-induced riots, tax disturbances, and demonstrations. This commission directly linked these disturbances to the marketing boards. The government made the following improvements based on recommendations of the commission. First, prices to producers are now fixed by the head of state (with the advice of technical officers) and no longer by individual marketing boards. Second, export duties on marketing boards produce were abolished, which brings in more money to pay farmers. Third, produce taxes imposed by state government are limited to 10%. Since the states would lose revenue, the federal military government is to make good any loss incurred, which it can easily do through the phenomenally increased revenue from petroleum. Fourth, the federal military government also is to meet any losses incurred by the marketing boards if the price to producers is fixed at a level which results in losses to the marketing boards. These reforms did not abolish the marketing boards, but improved their operational efficiency. The boards still pay the farmers, but the function of fixing prices has been eliminated.

By implication, farmers would be subsidized from general taxation in years of poor world prices, and there would no longer be a case for withholding part of their crop earnings in a good year in order to subsidize earnings in years of bad world prices. A high proportion of revenue earned from a wasting asset, oil, is to be spent on expanding a more permanent base of the economy: agriculture.

Have riots and disturbances substantially declined? Data presented in Table 3.9 shows that declared trade disputes have declined by more than 100%, from an average of 600 annually in the two-year period from 1964 to 1965 to about 180 between 1970 and 1973. The high figures for number of strikes and worker days lost in 1971 and early 1972 resulted from the inability of many firms in the private sector to pay workers the amount recommended by the Adebo Commission. In fact, the commission has brought about a structural change in the income structure by attempting to harmonize public and private sectors of the economy. It is only surprising that there were not more strikes and trade disputes in that period.

Table 3.9
Labor Relations and Riot Events in Nigeria

	1964	1965	1966	1967	1968	1969	1970	1971	1972	1973
Number of declared trade disputes	968	308	211	----	----	190	181	188	164	
Number of strikes	798	133	91	----	----	45	49	130	51	
Number of workers involved in strike action	217,100	36.201	28,035	----	----	8,837	16,480	67,057	39,208	
Number of worker-days lost as a result of strike action	984.852	164.142	112,901	----	----	19,194	37,386	173,057	133,900	
Number of farmer originated riots	3 (48 people killed)	8 (76 people killed)	----	----	----	----	2	2	1	
Other riot events (Tax, etc.)	15	82 (over 1000 killed)	----	----	----	----	6	3	2 10 killed	
Number of protest demonstrations	93	78	----	----	----	----	20	8	5	

Sources: Annual Reports and Statement of Accounts of the Central Bank of Nigeria : West Africa Magazine (1964–1966 and 1970 to 1973 weekly issues); Daily Times of Nigeria; Abstract of Statistics, Federal Office of Statistics, Lagos, Nigeria.

Farmer-originated riots have also declined substantially, and other riot disturbances have displayed a remarkable downward trend. The downward trend shows marked progress between 1970 and 1973. The number of trade disputes, strikes, and so on in the era of military rule shows that use of physical force cannot stop such events. Farmers' groups are happy with the new deal and are thus not motivated to cause disturbances.[45]

The military moved forcefully, directing its policies towards weak areas of the economy and the polity, and displaying evidence of mature judgment based on expert advice. The dependence on a bureaucratic mode of operation, and its attempt to reestablish order and discipline in the body polity reflects its organizational background.

Even though the government's no-strike order was in effect, it had to backdown in the face of a wave of strikes early in 1971. At the same time, the government prevented a few trade-union leaders from leaving the country by seizing their passports. The arrest of newspaper reporters followed and has continued sporadically. But in number and intensity, this does not compare to the repressive measures taken by the civilian party system in 1964 and 1965, or to the preventive detention act promulgated, but not carried through, by the party system, under which citizens would have lost their freedom without trial. The Nigerian military government has been far more tolerant than the civilian government. This does not excuse military action which, in any case, does not enhance its public image.

Opinions have differed as to the military government's decision to publicly execute armed robbers. It has been characterized as a repressive measure. In fact, since 1970, 210 convicted men have been so executed, including army officers, some of them convicted on charges of corruption. The military is oriented toward order and discipline, but essentially, this process serves a symbolic function of purification, by which the military appears to be a body which intends to cleanse the system of corruption. However, the wave of armed robbery which followed the end of the war and was allegedly perpetrated by runaway, armed soldiers has subsided. Even though this has succeeded in the short run, it represents a unidimensional way of solving the problem. Many people commit armed robbery because they are poor, lack employment, or have nothing to eat while they perceive fellow citizens riding in luxurious cars. We asked people, randomly, their view of this military action. Most reported that the highways were unsafe after the war and they were happy that this danger was substantially reduced.

In conclusion, industrial unrest, mob violence, and political assassinations have substantially declined over the number that occurred during the multiparty regime, due to effective policy decisions taken by the military government to correct the imbalance of income differentials and rural-urban development differentials.

POLITICAL INSTRUMENTS AND POLITICAL REFORMS

Youth Corps

The federal military government established the Nigerian Youth Corps in June 1973 with two specific aims: to inculcate in the youth a sense of service, discipline, dedication, national pride, and consciousness through nationally-directed programs; and to make Nigerian youth a potential instrument of national unity which would cut across political, social, religious, state, and ethnic loyalty.

The Youth Corps was initially recruited from among university graduates, but the program is expected to expand to cover all youth of college age. Members are transferred to projects in areas outside of their state of origin. They undergo paramilitary training, as well as learn the language, culture, and traditions of the community in which they work. This program parallels, in some respects, the activities of the American Peace Corps in Nigeria. The Nigerian Youth Corps works in the rural areas and thus constitutes a strong political instrument. Besides serving on community projects, the corps will also explain governmental policies to the rural communities. If it succeeds, it may bring the government to the people and reduce the influx of people from rural to urban centers.

What significance does the Youth Corps program have with respect to overall national development? Janowitz stated that if the military is to succeed in governing a civilian polity, it has to develop visible political instruments to generate political support for its programs.[46] Though this is one important reason for creating the Youth Corps, one cannot yet evaluate the success of this project because it is too recent a development. However, one can compare patterns of organization and management of the Youth Corps program and its relation to the military aims, the nature of the tasks to be performed, and its character and degree of involvement with the masses.

In Guinea, where Sékou Touré is the leader, a people's militia has been established, not as competitor of the military, but as a supplementary force to it. Organized as a direct arm of the "service civique," on a workplace basis, it is not perceived as a threat by the regular military. This program has succeeded where the Ghanaian Worker's Brigade failed. The Ghanaian Worker's Brigade was separate from the army until two years before the military coup which overthrew Nkrumah in 1966. The regular military perceived the Worker's Brigade as a rival organization and worked towards its final collapse.[47]

In 1964, Kenya established a National Youth Corps, comprised largely of well-seasoned former Mau-Mau guerilla fighters. But even with that background, the Youth Corps could not match the training and discipline of the Kenyan military. When, in 1966, attempts were made to recruit military officers from the Youth Corps on a quota basis, not enough suitable material could be found. This youth service was never able to provide an alternative to the army, which always commanded greater respect and prestige. The Zambian Youth Service collapsed for the same reasons. It is important that the youth corps program be organized as part of the military, or integrated into it, for two reasons: the military would not perceive it as an alternative and threat; and it would probably command as much respect as the military itself does, attracting suitable personnel, as well as providing a recruiting base for the military officer corps.[48]

The Tanzanian example is illustrative of the attempt to link party operations, the national youth corps, and the military in a new effort at nation bulding after the 1964 army mutiny. The youth service gradually became the army reserve as a result of the paramilitary training given to the service members in an integrated program with the military. The Tanzanian example is similar to the Israeli situation, where the Gadna preceded the Nahal in the Israeli army. Nigeria is one of an extremely few nations where the military took it upon itself to organize a youth program aimed at national mobilization. No one knows now whether the Nigerian youth program will be used as a recruiting base for the military. However, because it is an outgrowth of military planning, it will not be considered a rival organization by the military.[49]

The Tanzanian youth program is also succeeding because it has specific objectives in engineering and agriculture. While in Nigeria most of the members of the Youth Corps are engaged in teaching, there are divisions of agriculture and engineering. The division of agriculture is integrated with the extension services of the government ministry of agriculture in order to bring improved methods to the peasants. The Ghanaian youth program (Worker's Brigade) failed because it was designed as a safety valve for the release of political energy and as an instrument to harass the opposition. Lee has commented that since the Ghanaian Worker's Brigade had low achievement standards, it could not attain parity in prestige with the national security forces.[50]

The aims and mode of organization of the youth service programs are seen to be important determinants of their level of achievement, and also whether or not the corps is fully involved with the masses of the people.

The Nigerian youth service program has more than a fair chance of providing a base of support for the federal military government. In addition to the Youth Corps, new political experiments aimed at reaching down to the grass roots are being tried out in parts of the nation.

Local Government Reforms

Structural changes have been made in local government administration in some states of Nigeria. The most prominent is in Western Nigeria, where local councils have been merged to make them more financially viable and, thus, more capable of performing their duties. Many councils were created during the civilian-party regime to obtain political support from locally influential men who stood to gain by the creation of such councils. Local councils especially proliferated in those sections of the community where the party in power received most support. Such economically unviable councils became dependent on the state government for funds in order to perform their day-to-day statutory functions. Yet merging these councils would have cost the party in power tremendous loss of support. In an editorial, the *West Africa* commented that the merger of the councils was a bold political step which probably could have been taken only by a military regime. "In the heyday of party politics, such an action could not have been conceived let alone executed without unpleasant consequences."[51] Rather than regulate the demand for more viable councils, civilian politicians tended to encourage the status quo for selfish reasons. With the great coordination of activities, the councils have become more effective in performing their statutory functions.

Has this coordination of activities removed the government further from the people? The military government of Western Nigeria prevented such isolation by establishing area committees made up of local people. About 350 such committees have been created for the people of Western Nigeria. Because of this reform, the earlier practice, through which special committees—such as those responsible for education and health—dealt directly with various departments of a council, has been abolished, since it tended to fragment responsibility in council management. Such responsibilities have now been taken over by the newly-established committees, which bring more people from hitherto neglected parts of the state into government. One of the duties of the new committees is to collect taxes, which will henceforth be spent in the locality rather than spent to develop provincial capitals.

This bold action reduced the rural-urban gap and, particularly, brought the government to the grass roots level. In civilian-party days, the direct effects of government were felt in the rural areas only during shock raids by tax collectors, or when the party in power was campaigning for political support. The *West Africa* editorial mentioned earlier summarized the changes: "A new era in local government has dawned on Western Nigeria . . . an effective link should have been forged between the government and the governed."[52]

One distinctive effort of military politics, then, is to regulate demands for more councils by visibly moving to merge those that already exist. While fostering a democratic grass-roots politics, the military sought to coordinate policies at a higher level. It compensated for the complaints resulting from the loss of influence of a few local councillors by creating area councils that involved more people on a wider range of issues. Again, the military coordinates and centralizes policy making, but allows for decentralization of initiatives at the local level. This compensatory mechanism is exactly what permits such contradictory steps as centralization and decentralization to be achieved simultaneously. The directness of the military's move toward political reform and the creation of the Youth Corps program illustrates the military's determination to correct the imbalances inherited upon its accession to power.

An intriguing aspect of the reform is the new role assigned to the traditional rulers. The Obas and their chiefs will participate in the area committee decisions and constitute their own chieftaincy committees. As an expression of the faith of the military government in the traditional institution, this move contrasts sharply with the low prestige and role allocated to the chiefs by the civilian politicians. General Gowon, as Nigerian head of state said that he would be the last to advocate the scrapping of traditional institutions. This new role for the chiefs emphasizes the new direction of the political structure, which is attempting to cope more adequately with its tasks. Zolberg argued that in the developing African nations, the visible modern "political institutions, such as the political parties and groups, central executive and legislative bodies, as well as the apparatus of territorial administration (which often includes party structure) deal only with a portion of the total allocative activity. The remainder must be allocated by other means and other structures."[53] He further argued that, since modern institutions have shown little capacity to carry the load of development (party structure collapsed in Nigeria in 1966), there is always a residual sector of relatively traditional political activity that is not touched. In the context of this argument, the reforms undertaken by the military government, particularly the new role allocated to the traditional institutions, assume great significance. Earlier, we argued that the authority of the chiefs is vital to the establishment of governmental links with the peasant masses. Because they often bypassed the traditional institutions, the politicians always failed to reach this residual sector. This neotraditionalism or "patrimonialism" has been an important mechanism by which the military has reached down to the grass roots.

NOTES

1. Coleman, J., and Rosberg, C., *Political Parties and National Integration in Tropical Africa* (Berkeley, 1964), p. 9. See also L. Binder who conceives of national integration as a process of creating intra-state consensus, especially in bridging the elite-mass gap, in "National Integration and Political Development," *American Political Science Review* 57: 622-63.
2. Haas, E., *The Uniting of Europe: Political, Social and Economic Forces* (Stanford, 1958), p. 16.
3. Ibid., p. 118.
4. Etzioni, Amitai, *Political Unification — A Comparative Study of Leaders and Forces* (New York, 1965), p. 6.

5. De Vree, J.K., *Political Integration: The Formation of a Theory and its Problems* (The Hague, 1972), p. 118. Etzioni, *Political Unification.*

6. Etzioni, A., *The Active Society: A Theory of Societal and Political Processes* (London, 1968), p. 564.

7. This formulation is an adaptation from De Vree, *Political Integration*, p. 344.

8. See Map 4.1.

9. Deutsch, K., "On Communication Model in the Social Sciences," *Public Opinion Quarterly* 16: 356-380. See also Coleman, J., "Loss of Power," *American Sociological Review,* January, 1973.

10. Deutsch, K., "Communication Theory and Political Integration," in P. Jacob and T. Toscano, eds., *The Integration of Political Communities* (Philadelphia, 1964), pp. 46-74. See also Etzioni, *The Active Society,* p. 559; and De Vree, *Political Integration,* p. 346-49.

11. De Smith, C., "Federalism, Human Rights and the Protection of Minorities," in W. Currie, ed., *Federalism in the New Nations of Africa* (Chicago, 1964), p. 288.

12. Wheare, K.C., *Federal Government* (New York, 1951), pp. 35-36.

13. Ibid. De Smith, "Federalism," p. 288.

14. Watts, R.C., *Administration in Federal Systems* (London, 1970), pp. 73-89.

15. Wheare, *Federal Government.*

16. De Smith, "Federalism."

17. Winter, K.C., *Blueprints for Independence* (1961), pp. 55-61.

18. Lipset, "Some Social Requisites of Democracy"; Horowitz, *Three Worlds,* ch. 12; Weiner, "Political Participation and Political Development," in M. Weiner, ed., *Modernization;* Coleman and Rosberg, *Political Integration.*

19. Watts, *Administration,* ch. 12.

20. From an interview with the Midwestern State Commissioner for Education (August 29, 1972).

21. From an interview with the Permanent Secretary, Ministry of Economic Planning and Reconstruction, Western State (August 1972).

22. From an interview with Permanent Secretary, Ministry of Establishment, Western State (August 1972).

23. Deutsch, K., *Political Community and the North Atlantic Area— International Organization in the Light of Historical Experience* (Princeton, 1957), p. 90. For similar views on the self sustained growth of institutions, see Wheare, *Federal Government,* p. 237; Eisenstadt, S., *The Political System of Empire—The Rise and Fall of the Historical Bureaucratic Society* (New York, 1963), p. 25; Russett, B., "Toward a Model of Competitive International Politics," in J.N. Rosenau, ed., *International Politics and Foreign Policy—A Reader in Research and Theory* (New York, 1969), pp. 119-30; and Galtung, J., "On the Failure of the International System," *Journal of Peace Research* 1 (1967): 95-119.

24. *West Africa,* May 1973.

25. ECA Report, United Nations Headquarters, February 1973.

26. Watts, *Administration,* ch. 6.

27. Coleman and Rosberg, *Political Integration.*

28. Deutsch, *Political Community.*

29. Ibid.

30. Deutsch, K., "Large and Small States in the Integration of Large Political Communities," in International Political Science Association, *Proceedings* (Stockholm, 1955), p. 3.

31. Watts, *Administration,* ch. 6.

32.   Interview, Permanent Secretary, Military Governor's Office.
33.   Watts, *Administration*, Ch. 6.
34.   *Daily Times*, May 7, 1973.
35.   *Daily Times*, May 12, 1973.
36.   Watts, *Administration*.
37.   Budget Speech by the Head of State of Nigeria, Federal Ministry of Information, April 1973.
38.   Interview with the Military Attache, Nigerian Embassy, Washington, D.C., July 1973.
39.   First Interim Report on the National Development Plan, Lagos, Nigeria, June 1972.
40.   Pye, L., "Burmese Army in Politics," in J.J. Johnson, *The Role of the Military in Underdeveloped Nations* (Princeton, 1962).
41.   Edelman, M. *The Symbolic Uses of Politics* (Urbana, Ill., 1967).
42.   *West Africa*, May 1973.
43.   Budget Speech, Military Governor of the Lagos State of Nigeria, April 1972.
44.   First Interim Report on the National Development Plan.
45.   *West Africa*, June 1973.
46.   Janowitz, M., *The Military in the Political Development of Nations* (Chicago, 1964).
47.   Lee, J.M., *African Armies and Civil Order* (New York, 1969).
48.   Ibid.
49.   Ibid.
50.   Ibid.
51.   *West Africa*, February 5, 1973.
52.   Ibid.
53.   Zolberg, A., "Military Intervention in the New States of Africa," in Bienen, H., ed., *The Military Intervenes* (Chicago, 1970).

Chapter 4
Resource Allocation and the Structure of Power in Nigeria

What specific problems face a federal system of government in Nigeria? What is the distribution of functions, responsibilities, and resources between the federal government, on the one hand, and regional/state governments on the other? In what ways are such arrangements changing under different political systems, and with what effects? In this chapter, an attempt will be made to show that under the party system, the federal government was unable to carry out purposeful, nationally-oriented programs of economic and social development because of the organizational structure of power distribution. The present military-bureaucratic system has, on the contrary, moved to take greater control of strategic areas of policy and to show greater ability to manage national affairs. A second effort will show that, while the allocation of resources under the party system was haphazard, unstable, and inadequate, more effective policies are being pursued by the present federal military government, with a resultant increased stability in the structure of relationships, higher income for the federal government, and greater leverage in its control of national affairs.

There is no one formula for the operation of a federal system in terms of functions, responsibilities, and revenue, although certain basic criteria operate among the older British Commonwealth federal systems, Canada, and Australia.[1] Among the criteria is fiscal independence, by which each separate government is given power to raise, mobilize, and spend resources according to the functions it is to perform. Fiscal independence, if mismanaged, may impair overall national development through uncoordinated mobilization of resources and expenditure. In

Nigeria between 1960 and 1966, the regional government systematically reduced the nation to a confederation of powerful little nations. Another criteria is efficiency, where powers to tax and perform selected functions are allocated to specific governments capable of most rationally administering them, and where industrial projects are located in the most economically suitable sites. However, what is most rational and efficient may not be most politically acceptable. Thus, efficiency must be reconciled with what is politically acceptable, if the bases of distribution are to be perceived as equitable.

These principles are oftentimes in combination with another, and the choice of action varies with local contingencies of economic, political, and social forces from federation to federation. In Nigeria, in the making of the constitutions, policy areas are divided among the federal (central) and regional state governments. In the following pages, we will examine this distribution of functions and critically evaluate how the distribution has hampered or enhanced the operation of a federal system.

ALLOCATION OF FUNCTIONS AND RESPONSIBILITIES

The 1954 federal constitution created three lists of functions and areas of responsibility.

1. *Exclusive list.* There were 43 areas under the authority of the federal government, including banking, company regulation and taxation, transportation and communication of nationwide importance, public debts and borrowing, mines and minerals, matters affecting the federal territory of Lagos, census, nationality and security, advanced research of nationwide importance (with reference to primary productions and mineralogy), and maintenance of the already existing institutions of higher learning.
2. *Concurrent list.* Areas jointly managed by both the federal and the state authorities (a kind of "twilight zone") included higher education, health, industrial development, labor and industrial relations, statistics, and water resources.
3. *Residual list.* Areas over which regional or state governments had absolute jurisdiction include primary and secondary education, health, local government, intraregional transportation, and housing.

The lists above reveal several weaknesses in the intergovernmental allocation of functions.

First, the very length of the concurrent list impaired the federal government's ability to give a sense of direction to the national economy. The inclusion of industrial development on this list encouraged the duplication of industrial projects (for instance cement manufacturing) and the consequent wastage of scarce resources. Even though cement production in the country is still below demand, the overhead cost of building several new plants in various regions has increased cost to the consumer (price of locally-produced cement being sometimes higher than that for the imported). The insured competitiveness of imported cement was one factor in the decline of the industry. A more efficient approach would have been the expansion of only one or two plants with consequent reduction in overhead costs.

The attraction of foreign investment toward the establishment of local industrial projects highlights the very unhealthy competition among the different regions/states. For lack of an overall policy, richer areas were able to attract investors into their states. Consequently, the poorer states offered inordinately attractive incentives, in terms of how much profit could be repatriated and what government share of participation would be demanded of investors. The situation degenerated so severely that foreign investors were sometimes unwilling to face the choice of one over the other and started demanding that the federal government take steps to coordinate all efforts in this direction. The leader of the British Confederation of Industries said: "It would be an advantage if the procedure for obtaining approval for new industrial investment or expansion could be clarified ideally by the provision of a *single point of reference with property authority*"[2] (our italics). The ludicrously embarrassing situation revealed the weakness of a federal system in which the regions had become all but separate nations. It could be argued, though, that the federal government had control over strategic areas of policy. For instance, its full control of transportation and communication was of crucial importance in determining the level of domestic as well as foreign trade activities, with special reference to the production of exports and the level of importation. Secondly, its powers extended over the kind of financial institutions that were established. This meant that it had influences over capital mobilization for the public sector and for general national development. Again, since it was in control of foreign policy, it could control the supply of foreign aid (until recently, a critically vital support of the economy). Where foreign aid emanates from and how it will be utilized is an integral part of foreign policy.

It would seem, therefore, that the power of the federal government was greater than what is at first imagined. But why did it not seize upon this apparent advantage and manipulate itself into a position of power? The answer lies, in part, in the power orientation of the regional and federal level politicians. While the regional politicians were attempting to consolidate their powers in their respective regions, they were being tacitly encouraged by federal level politicians, since they in turn, depended for political support on the same sources and constituencies. The character of politics thus encouraged a situation which invidiously undermined real federalism. What more need was there for a new kind of system that would purposefully reassert federal powers, but at the same time reaffirm state autonomy?

Even though the federal government in prewar times had jurisdiction over banking, money, and foreign policy, the residual list removed specific policy areas of development from the federal government. This rendered it ineffectual in planning a national economy. For instance, secondary education, which feeds the universities, needed to be, at the very minimum, a concurrent subject so that overall training at the university level could be more adequately planned and executed.

Secondly, the training and control of higher manpower supply — a very sensitive area politically and economically — was inadequately handled. The regions, and now the states engage in cutthroat competition in the effort to establish universities and higher technical colleges. Several problems stand in the way of such efforts. Many of the states are poor and lack the financial means. There is dearth of qualified faculty, and the cost of inviting overseas faculty is prohibitive. The solution does not reside in duplicating existing facilities in a process of unhealthy competition, but in streamlining supply and channelling efforts into the needed areas. Therefore, the need for a more coordinated higher-education policy is compelling. With the proliferation of state-government white paper establishing universities or higher technical colleges (which often served as camouflaged nuclei of full university systems), the federal military government moved in to remove higher education from the concurrent list and place it on the exclusive list. This step thus properly recognized higher education as a codeterminant of national growth and, therefore, not of mere local importance. However, this and other similar steps must be taken with a recognizable demonstration of good faith on the part of the federal government. Where such steps are taken with the tacit intention of weakening state governments, they carry with them dangers of political overtones in an ethnically plural society. It is being suggested that, while federal government lays down broad principles, the states should have the autonomy of interpreting the broad details of such policies.

Table 4.1 shows the shift that has taken place in the allocation of functions between federal and state governments.

What changes can be noted? External affairs, higher education, and trade union affairs have moved into the exclusive list. The three policy areas are of strategic national importance, as argued in the case of higher education. Between 1960 and 1965, each regional government established foreign missions abroad (although only at the consular level). Nigeria did not only possess an uncoordinated national foreign policy, but it was easy to see that the different consulates in the different foreign capitals were competing against each other. The abolition of these separate consular agencies by the military government gave the nation a coherent national image in foreign matters. The reason given for moving trade union activities into the exclusive list was not to exercise control over union activities but to coordinate and purposefully unite these unions, which are hopelessly divided along capitalist (AFL-CIO affiliated) and socialist (affiliated) lines.

Table 4.1 also reveals that public order, industrial development, planning, and utilities have come more under federal authority, although the rights of states are respected in those areas. Also, housing and health are still recognized as local matters, although we recommend that health become a national matter. One striking feature is that the areas on the concurrent list have been reduced. In general, the larger the number of policy areas on the concurrent list, the less efficient the operation of the federal system tends to be.

PROBLEMS WITH REVENUE ALLOCATION

The present federal military government has employed the disparity between fiscal needs and the revenue sources of the states as a principal means of assuming powers to which it did not originally have claim. This approach is reinforced by the fact that most of the states are only recently created and have no fiscal precedents on which to base any claims, or probably even any resentment of federal moves. But first it must be shown (as was assumed in the opening sentence of this section), that the states are indeed highly dependent upon their share of federal revenue allocation and would hardly have been viable otherwise. Table 4.4 shows that federal allocation to regions/states has always been more than 50% of total revenue of such regions/states, and it would have been impossible for such states or regions to operate without the allocation.

Besides, the states or regions have been run on a budget deficit, as the figures in Table 4.4 reveal; the differences have been made up either by special appropriation to the states or more often by grants from the federal government. It should be understood, however, that this allocation to the states is based on constitutional statutes and is not done simply by the "grace" or the "goodwill" of the federal government. But the argument is that the federal government could increasingly manipulate itself into a systematically stronger position. The question then becomes: why was this opportunity not taken advantage of during multiparty times but taken advantage of during the military regime?

The answer is consistent with the position already taken that the parties were too busy consolidating their strengths in their states of origin and, moreover, did not perceive the federal or central government as a position

Table 4.1
Distribution of Legislative and Executive Authorities
in Nigeria

Policy Areas	1963-65	1970-73
External Affairs	ER	E
Defence	E	E
Public Order	C	ER
Elections	E	E
Finance:		
Foreign exchange	E	E
Currency and coinage	E	E
Foreign loans	ER	ER
Taxes		
Customs and Excise	E	E
Personal Income	ER	ER
Banking	E	E
External Trade	ER	ER
Industries	C	ER
Mines and oil field	E	E
Planning (Economic and social)	C	ER
Communications and Transportation	E	E
Utilities (electricity)	C	ER

Policy Areas	1963-65	1970-73
Education		
Elementary & secondary	R	R
University	C	E
Health	R	R
Labor and Industrial Relations:		
Trade Unions	C	E
Industrial disputes	C	C
Housing	R	R

*Under 1963 Constitution.

Sources: R.L Watts New Federation   (Claredon Press,
    Oxford 1966) pp. 364-366; Federal gazette of
    Nigeria (weekly).

Explanation of notations: E = Exclusive

C = Concurrent

R = Residual

Notes: Where the Federal power is more restricted
    than the letter   E, it is shown as ER to
    indicate that certain aspects of that
    subject are placed under regional or state
    authority,   or that the consent of the
    state or region for the exercise of
    Federal authority in such policy area
    is required. EC indicates that Federal
    government has overall coordination
    authority, while regional governments
    have autonomous power over their own
    area concerns.

Table 4.2
System of Revenue Allocation to the Regions/States
of Nigeria Since 1954

Year of Introduction	Commission	Principles	System of Allocation
1954/5	Chick	Derivation Fiscal autonomy	50% of import and excise duties on tobacco, and 100% of import duties on motor fuel, according to consumption 50% of other impor duties (other than on alcohol, tobacco, and motor fuel 100% of income tax (except on companies) according to residence. 100% mining rents and royalties, according to extraction 50% export duties, according to origin
1959/60	Raisman Trees	Fiscal autonomy Derivation Unified national policy	100% of import and excise duties on tobacco, and 100% of import duties on motor fuel, according to consumption. 100% export duties, according to origin 50% mining rents and royalties, according to extraction 30% of other import duties (other than on alcohol, tobacco, and motor fuel), and 30% of mining rents and royalties, to be

Year of Introduction	Commission	Principles	System of Allocation
			paid into the Distributable Pool Account: North, 40/95; West, 24/95; East, 31/95.
1966/7	Binns	Derivation Fiscal autonomy Unified national policy	100% of import and excise on tobacco and motor fuels, according to consumption 100% export duties, according to origin 50% mining rents and royalties, according to extraction 35% of other import duties, and 35% of mining rents and royalties, to be paid into the Distributable Pool Account: East, 30% West, 20% Mid-West, 8% North 42%.
1968/9		An interim system pending the working out of a new revenue system following the creation of 12 states	As above, except that the Pool Account is to be distributed as follows: Each of the six Northern States (kano, North-Western, North-Central, North-Eastern, kwara, Benue-Plateau) 7% Western 18%, Lagos, 2%, Mid-Western, 8%, East-Cental 17.5%, South Eastern, 7.5% River, 5%.
1969/70		Also an interim system pending a new constitution	100% of import and excise duties on motor fuel, and 100% of excise duty of tobacco, according to consumption 60% export duties, according to origin 45% of mining rents and royalties according to extraction 35% of other import duties, 40% of export duties, 50% of mining rents and royalties, and 50% of excise duties on tobacco, to be distributed as follows: 50% equally among the States, and 50% among them according to population.

of strength. The orientation was towards nibbling at the center, which was the source of all "goods." In contrast, the military aimed at correcting such imbalance. Indeed, the first military government proceeded immediately upon accession to office to cancel federalism and establish a unitary system of government. This failed. The present government learned from that error and immediately reinstituted the federal system. General Gowon, the present head of state asserted in 1966 that only a federal system with a strong center, and states which have a certain measure of autonomy, can fulfill the hopes of a united Nigeria.

The military organizational characteristics of bureaucratic coordination and order and hierarchical authority can be seen to be in operation. Table 4.4 reveals (1) that in 1972 and 1973, total federal allocation to states was about three times the 1965 figures — an important factor by which the federal government could dictate its terms; (2) that total allocation to the states constituted a decreasing proportion of total federal revenue, while the amount allocated more than trebled (this shows that the federal government's revenue is increasing phenomenally); (3) that allocation to the states constituted more than one-half of state/regional revenue and that this proportion increased from 65% to over 80%. The significance of this is that these political units are heavily dependent on this source and are increasingly so, thus revealing the measure of federal strength.

Also revealed are its aim in assuming power as well as its ability to learn on the job. The history of party rule from 1960 through 1965 was marked by a kind of brinkmanship in interethnic competition — a situation which can hardly be characterized as stable.

Table 4.4 also reveals that the federal shares of revenue allocated to regions/states increased phenomenally (sources of increase will be considered later) when the military came to power. For instance, in any year since 1971, it has doubled what was allocated to these political units in 1965 (last year of civilian rule). At a time of consolidation, a massive allocation of revenue to the states serves to structure orientation to the federal center as a source of authority. The interest of each state is toward getting more money from the center, and thus, they are often willing to dance to the tune dictated by the center. In this exchange situation, the federal government gains in power and prestige what it loses in money.[3] Increased revenue is the instrument with which the federal government maneuvers itself into stronger power positions.

If revenue allocation has been so critically vital to the survival of the regions/states (and if it is remembered that the boundaries of these political units are often coterminous with the geographical location of ethnic groups), sensitivity and volatility of this subject can be appreciated. As the principal bone of contention among the various states, and between them and the federal government, it has been a chief source of

Table 4.3
Current Arrangement for Revenue Allocation (1971/72)
Derived from Statutory Regulations and Decrees

Type of Tax	Federal Govt.	States	Distribu- table Pool Account	Remarks
Statutory Allowance.				
Import Duty				
Tobacco	–	On basis of consumption by state	–	The duty on petro- leum products is 1/11d per gallon.
Motor Spirit }1/9d per } gallon } Diesel oil }	1/11d	On basis of consumption by state	–	
Motor Spirit }2d per } gallon Diesel oil		–	100%	Authority Decree No. 13 of 1970 and Legal Notice No. 25 of 1969.
Unspecified	65%	–	35%	
Wine Beer, spirits	100%	–	–	
Export Duties Produce, Hides and skins	–	2/3 on basis of derivation i.e. 60% on basis of deri- vation, 86% of 1/3	40% of 1/3 = 131/3%	Decree No. 13 of 1970 Customs Tariff No. 27 09/10.
Excise Duties Tobacco) Motor spirit)) Diesel Oil) Unspecified)	50%	–	50%	
Mining Royalties and rents :				
Offshored	100%	–		
Insured	5%	45% to state of origin		Decree No 9 1971.

Table 4.4
Regional/State Shares of Federal Statutory Allocations:
1962-65, 1970-73

All Regions/States of
Nigeria

Year	Total N million	%	% of all Fed. Rev.	% of all Reg. / State Rev.	% of all Nigerian Revenue
1962/3	46.9	100	40.7	65.4	33.5
1963/4	48.8	100	39.2	68.8	33.3
1964/5	50.7	100	33.9	68.0	29.2
1965/6	63.8	100	39.6	71.4	34.3
1970/1	114.7	100	35.2	79.4	31.1
1971/2	143.4	100	30.5	78.6	24.3
1972/3	174.7	100	27.9	81.2	23.2

political instability. There are statutory provisions for the sharing of the revenue, but these provisions or formulas have had to be constantly revised as a result of political pressure from the regions prior to December 1965.

In what ways did the party system handle the problem of sharing revenue and with what impact on political stability and economic development? What changes has the military government made and with what results? The history of revenue allocation statutory laws dates back to 1946, but we will begin from 1954 when a federal system was instituted. Even though the period from 1954 to 1961 is not generally indicated in this study, it is important to go back in time for continuity. Before that, certain general points need be made.

Explicit criteria must guide whatever formula would be arrived at. Such criteria are: the principles of *derivation, even progress, national interest, fiscal autonomy, need,* and *unified national policy.* The principle of derivation states that a region or state is statutorily entitled to all revenues that are capable of being identified as having originated from, or being attributable to, such a region or state. Such a principle, on the face of it, appears equitable because each region or state is entitled to what it contributed to the total revenue. However, it is important that each region's resources be identifiable through adequate data collection. This requirement was not always fulfilled.[4] This principle, however, had the effect of increasing the wealth of the richer states (since they had more adequate means and resources to expand economically), and at the same time, of starving the more needy regions. The net effect was to increase the disparity and insure political instability.

Performance of Party System

A new fiscal commission (the Raisman Commission) was appointed in 1959 and 1960 to review the fiscal position. It was guided by the principals of derivation and fiscal autonomy. Fiscal autonomy requires that each region/state be given fiscal power and independence to raise its own taxes in order to perform its duties and remain autonomous. This principle runs counter, at several points, to the principle of unified national policy. The joint operation of both principles of derivation and fiscal autonomy could only encourage regional separatism, and the abrogation of a national orientation and accountability. Indeed, both principles agree basically in spirit with the wide autonomous powers constitutionally allocated to the regions in 1954. It is little wonder that the federal system was founded on a weak center, against which the regions were separately and sometimes jointly seen to work.

As a consequence, the disparity between the regions was widened and the seeds of a south-north (richer-poorer) confrontation already laid. By 1960, the regions received 40% of all revenues raised in the country, as opposed to 22% received earlier. The Western region (which had cocoa, a high-selling commodity in the world market at the time) started to enjoy a period of great fiscal boom. The North also recorded surpluses, while the East found it difficult to balance its recurrent budgets and was not in a position to undertake any major capital developments. The intriguing question is: why would the North and East agree to such an arrangement? Several answers can be offered. First, Nigeria was still not independent at the time. The North and East had to go along with the plans of the others, as well as those of the British colonial government. Second, the North had cotton, groundnuts, tin ore, and other resources and probably perceived, at the time, that it could base its development only on those resources. Third, and most significantly, each party sought by all means to consolidate itself in its own region. Any constitutional source of power that would guarantee that goal was most welcome. Indeed, overall national consideration was secondary to this overriding, narrowly local objective.

The overall result was that the fiscal position of the regions was strengthened while that of the federal government became progressively weaker. Simultaneously, the widening of the interregional gap caused furor in interstate relationships. The East, and to some extent the North, questioned the derivation principle, while the West thought the principle should be further expanded.

At Independence in 1959 and 1960, a newly-appointed commission (Raisman) was asked to include the principles of unified national policy, derivation, and fiscal autonomy. It is arguable whether this new design was to even out the disparity, or to rhetorically emphasize the newly independent status of Nigeria. In any case, it was a weak principle since it was capable of many interpretations. That is, it could have been made to subsume many other unspecified principles. Also, since it was not capable of quantitative expression, it might not even have served immediate needs created by political pressures.[5]

However, the Raisman Commission recommended an innovation: the establishment of a "Distributable Pool Account." This was similar to a development fund, into which a certain percentage of national revenue was to be ploughed. From this pool, revenue was to be allocated to the regions on the basis of need and national interest in the following ratio: North, 40; East, 31; West, 24. At once, it is seen that attempts were made to reduce the regional gap. The effectiveness of such innovation would depend, however, on what percentage of what was ploughed into this pool. As Table 4.2 shows, only 30% of "other import duties" (that is, other than alcohol etc.) and 30% of mining rents and royalties came into this pool. If it is realized that royalty on petroleum accounted for less than 0.5% of total revenue at that time, but now accounts for more than 75%, and that the military government had increased the proportion of the distributable pool 500 times to 50% of all such royalties, it will be appreciated why the states today are happier with the federal military government than the regions were with the multiparty federal system.

The principle of need was based on population as its chief index. While this appears an equitable criterion, need cannot be adequately determined without proper specification of statutory responsibilities. Need is a function of governmental responsibility. Even though all regional/state governments have the same responsibilities, sometimes this does not depend on population. Our position is that the criterion of population is too broad. It is, therefore, not surprising to see that the population census exercise has become a highly politicized, highly sensitive area of relationship. Indeed, the census exercise of 1962 was futile because figures were allegedly inflated. It generated such interethnic distrust and hostility that it was finally rejected. The 1963 census, which is currently being used, has also been severely criticized as inaccurate for the same reasons. The census problem was, indeed, one of the immediate causes of the civil strife from 1965 to 1970, since it underlined the north-south confrontation.[6]

The military government had been under pressure to revise the census figure, but did not start a new census exercise until May 1973. The chief reasons were to depoliticize the area as much as possible by letting hostilities subside, and to see that justice was being done. Moreover, the military government has made use of the bureaucrats and intellectuals (to design, plan, and execute the exercise) as well as the local chiefs (to explain the reasons to the people). Besides, the military government decreed that no police officers could be used for tax collection exercises then and in the future.[7] The concept of patrimonialism raised in the theoretical framework is seen to adequately explain this process. In fact, we are arguing that the military-bureaucratic structure is employing a neglected institution—the local chieftaincy—to perform its tasks. The relationship between political structures and the character of tasks to be performed is seen to be in more harmonious relationship than what obtained in multiparty times. At that time, chiefs were neglected and an unprecedented use was made of the police.

Performance Of The Military

A new fiscal commission was appointed in 1966 and 1967 since the Raisman formula had proven inadequate.[8] It was to be guided by the same three principles as above, but was requested to deemphasize the principle of derivation and also find means of reducing the interregional gap in development. It was also to insure that the federation as a whole helped the north "to the fullest extent possible to achieve greater measure of parity with the other regions."[9]

The most important highlight of the commission's report was the expansion of the Distributable Pool Account. Hitherto, only 30% of proceeds from mining rents and royalties of import duties were paid into this account, but this was expanded to 35%. Also, revenue accruing from excise duties on motor fuel was passed on to the states. The impact of these changes (all at the expense of the federal government) was truncated by the civil war and was further complicated by the creation of twelve states out of the existing four regions.

Between 1968 and 1969, the situation in the country was in a state of flux: the civil war was raging and the political structure of the country had been fundamentally altered by the creation of states. Even though the measures for revenue allocation were meant to be temporary, the problem of how to share the distributable account among 12 states emerged. The federal military government followed the precedent laid out by the party system in 1964 when a new region (the Midwest) was carved out of the Western region. This precedent was based on the criterion of population. This precedent was used to divide the shares of the West and East among the new states carved out of them on the basis of population.

However, the Northern region's share was divided equally among the six new northern states.

Even though this arrangement was temporary, it had an obvious weakness. The sharing of the former regional revenue among the new states into which it was divided carried with it the assumption that such states were still regarded as part of a regional block. This was particularly important with respect to the north. Similarly, employing the population criteria to divide finances provided the Eastern and Western regions carried the assumption that expenditure varied with population. In the Western region (from which the Midwest was created), recurrent expenditure decreased by only 11% while its population was reduced by 25%.

In fiscal year 1969-70, greater emphasis was placed on the principles of need and national interest, which further enlarged the distributable pool. The principle of derivation, by which 100% of export duties accrued to the state of origin was changed; now only 60% goes to the state and 40% goes to the distributable account. The military government has exhibited willingness to use the distributable account as an instrument to even out development. At the same time, the revenue going to the states (100%) from excise duty on tobacco was cancelled. Fifty per cent now goes to the distributable account and the remaner to the federal government.

The most significant development was the use of the distributable pool: 50% was to be shared equally among the states and the remaining 50% on the basis of population. Two things can be inferred from this: first, the principle of equity (50% shared equally) and fairness (population) is in operation; and second, conscious efforts are being made to shift political orientation to the national scene by emphasizing national interest and even development.

The interim arrangement of fiscal year 1971-72 (decree no. 9, 1971) improved on the 1969-70 arrangement by anticipating the increased revenue from oil. All offshore revenue from oil goes to the federal government.

The net effect of these changes has been: (1) the dependence of states on export duty revenue has been reduced. Export duties are an unreliable source of income due to the vagaries of world prices and the uncertainties of production. The military government thus ensures the financial stability of the states. (2) The absolute share of the revenue to the states has increased substantially, although the relative proportion of the total federal revenue is declining. This can only mean that federal revenue is increasing at a rate far greater than it was during the multiparty times, and that the federal military government has become financially stronger.

Taxation Powers

How has the present military government sought to increase the base of federal taxation powers or to alter its structure? How has it enhanced or diminished its financial status vis-a-vis the states and how does this compare with the position during the multiparty regime?

There are as many as 90 federal, local, or state sources of taxation. However, only 5 of these sources were important until the military assumed power. These were import, export, excise, company, and mining taxes, which jointly accounted for 75% of annual revenue before 1966. Other taxes, such as personal income tax, company income tax, capital gains tax, and so on, contribute only about 6% of total revenue.

The federal government has, from time to time, used import tariffs to raise revenue or manipulate the economy. Tax from this source is unstable (although it is substantial), as it could raise inflation and depress the market if overemphasized. Between 1967 and 1970, the federal government raised tariff on several goods since revenue, in general, was low. It lowered them on several goods, according to the budget speech of 1971 and 1972, since substantial revenue was coming in from other sources. In the 1972-73 budget speech, import duties on raw materials (manipulation for industrial purposes) and excise duties (to encourage local production) were reduced by 50%. Unlike the party government, the military has encouraged the importation of industrial wares and other goods, underlining the need for the diversification and broadening of the tax base.

The federal government's moves to share revenues from export duties with the states and put some of it in the Distributable Pool Account have, in part, reduced the states' dependence on this unstable source (while states are adequately compensated for such loss by increased federal aid from other sources). It has also shifted the balance of taxation power in favor of the federal government.

Personal Income Tax

Between 1963 and December 1965, revenue from personal income tax was about 2% of aggregate federal revenue. The federal military government sought to raise the income tax burden of the population and reduce allowances according to the provisions set down below: (1) reduction of personal allowances from 300 to 200 (1 = $2.80); (2) reduction of children's educational allowance from 190 to 90 per child and thus of overall children's allowance from 1,000 to 600; (3) increases in income rate and income tax rates for residents of the federal territory of Lagos; (4)

inclusion of housing allowance in taxable income; (5) uniform capital allowances for all forms of enterprises, corporate and noncorporate; and (6) capital gains tax of 20%. The income rate to be paid by every Lagos resident insures that taxpayers who avoid taxes by claiming allowances (which may, in total, exceed income) still contribute something to the federal revenue.

However, the burden of the taxes falls on the lower income group, whose tax burden has increased relative to the higher paid. For instance the (£N0-1,000) income groups shows an increase of 271% while a person who earns £N10,000 has an increase of only 4%. Since the majority of the people are in the former category, this step should bring increased revenue to the federal government. Again, the liability of the taxpayer who has one child has increased by 755%, the married without children by 400%, and the single by 271%.

This exercise was designed not only to raise more money but to discourage population increases. However, it raises ominous consequences for stability. Many of the lower income group who have many children are subject to the fullest impact of the new taxation. There have been no protests and demonstrations because Lagos (where this new system operates) is only one city, and the residents have paid lower personal taxes than many other parts of the country. Other new sources of revenue are the introduction of a 20% company super tax, and a capital gains tax by which dividends paid to Nigeria out of capital funds and of profits earned by a pioneer company from nonpioneer undertakings are taxed.

These new measures have raised the contribution of the personal, company, and other taxes to the federal revenue from 6% to more than 10%. Table 5.12 below reveals changes in the federal government's revenue from 1962 to 1973. As the figures indicate, revenue increased by more than 20%. The rate of growth during the multiparty regime was much lower than during the military regime. Even though oil has contributed substantially to this phenomenal rise, changes in the tax base and powers indicated have been highly significant. The evidence thus confirms the hypothesis that the federal military government is becoming financially stronger vis-a-vis the states than the multiparty system federal government was vis-a-vis the regions.

This hypothesis agrees with the observation in many of the other commonwealth federations. Birch has observed that in an efficient federal system, federal revenue grows faster than regional revenue.[10] In view of the assuredly increasing revenue, the federal military government has either to give more money to the states or take over more of their functions. It is doing both. Giving more aid to the states creates constitutional complexities. What principles govern aid to states? The government could base aid upon need, progress, national interest, matching principle, and so on, but it must be particularly careful, since injudicious selection of any of the above could lead to an inconsistent set of allocative criteria and open the federal government to charges of unfairness.

Apparently, the federal government has been employing an assumption of even progress. In 1969 and 1970, it authorized the grant of one million Naira to each of the nine states which have no governmental headquarters. The idea was to lay a basis for the autonomy of each state, so that it could be less dependent on the facilities of the older states. Thus, while the federal military government is acquiring more strategic functions, it is also establishing a basis for state autonomy (as can be appreciated in the revenue and tax allocation). This trend of action agrees with the military organizational characteristics of centralization of authority at the center and decentralization of initiatives described earlier.

Another way in which the federal military government uses its increasing powers is to depoliticize the location of industries. The location of the iron and steel industry became a bone of contention among the various regions.[11] The federal government declared that industries were to be located on the basis of economic viability, that is, on the principle of economic rationality. To induce acquiescence, it attempted to reconcile the rationality principle with what was politically acceptable by announcing at the same time that the government would disperse industrial projects. The nation was divided into industrial zones and several small-scale industries were set up in those areas that were neglected. Public attention was thus diverted from the highly politicized big project to the immediacy of smaller ones. Thus, by assuming resources are "divisible" and therefore "continuous," acquiescence was induced and stability maintained.

NOTES

1. See Wheare, K.C., *Federal Government* (London, 1957); Watts, Ronald, *Administration in Federal Systems* (London, 1970); Prest, Arthur, *Public Finance in Underdeveloped Countries* (London, 1962).
2. Confederation of British Industries Report, London and Lagos, 1971.
3. Bredemeier, Harry C., *Personality and Exchange Systems* (in press); Coleman, James, "Loss of Power," *American Sociological Review*, Jan. 1973.
4. See Phillips, Adedotun, "Nigeria's Federal Financial Experience," *Journal of Modern African Studies* 9 (1971): 389-408; Adedeji, Adebayo, *Nigerian Federal Finance* (New York, 1969).
5. Phillips, "Nigeria's," p. 391.
6. The recently released provisional figures have also raised such scepters of a

northern domination of the south. Debates have started on this issue in Nigerian newspapers since June 1974.

7. *West Africa,* April 1973.
8. Binns, K.J., *Report of the Fiscal Review Commission,* Federal Ministry of Information, Lagos, Nigeria, p. 34.
9. Phillips, "Nigeria's," p. 403.
10. Birch, A.H., "Intergovernmental Financial Relations in New Federations," in U.K. Hicks, ed. *Federalism and Economic Growth in Underdeveloped Countries: A Symposium.* (New York), 1961).
11. Aboyade, Oyetunji, "Relations Between Central and Local Institutions in the Development Process," in Arnold Riukin, ed., *Nations by Design* (New York, 1968), pp. 83-118.

Chapter 5
Economic Development
In Nigeria

Many observers have emphasized military ineptitude in handling problems of third-world economic development, arguing that the military's primary motive for intervening in politics is to insure its own corporate interests. Any economic development that takes place under military rule is said to be a secondary by-product. Nordlinger, for example, has insisted that the military's corporate interest rarely inclines them toward economic reform, which together with military values, goes a long way in accounting for the military's disinclination to match their original "*pronunciamentos*" with governmental decisions.[1] In this chapter, we shall show that, in Nigeria, the military has performed more efficiently than the party system with respect to economic development.

In Nigeria and elsewhere in Africa, the political party has been as much an interest group as the military. In Ghana, the Convention Peoples Party sought to insure its existence in all manner of ways (economic, political, and social) and particularly sought to preserve the power of the ruling hierarchy of the party system. The Action Group of Nigeria was reported to have used government money between 1960 and 1963 to expand its own activities in such large amounts that it seriously impaired economic development in Western Nigeria, where it was in power at the time. The Action Group party was hardly more guilty of this offense than any other major political party of that time. The criterion of interest-group politics, therefore, assumes importance in evaluating ruling groups in third world countries only as a measure of the relative motivation of alternative ruling groups. Characterization of interest-group behavior as an attribute of the military and not of the party system reveals a democratic bias. A fruitful area of sociological investigation, therefore, is to compare and contrast the relative significance of motivation toward corporate interest as an evaluative criterion of ruling groups. Probably more important are the ways in which the military has altered the structure of economic decision making, initiated and sustained a shift from one type of economy to the other, and altered the pattern of investment.

STRUCTURE OF ECONOMIC DECISION MAKING: IMPACT ON DEVELOPMENT

Since the early 1950s, economic development in third world countries has been promoted through a series of development plans aimed at consciously fostering the growth of various sectors of the economy. Nigeria has completed three such development plans in its history. As the sole instrument of economic development, the plans' success depends largely on the decision making that has gone into their construction. Such processes include the design of institutional decision-making bodies (who does it include, at what levels?), the institutional linkages of such bodies, and the nature of policy decisions such as the aim and the scope of operation. The elements enumerated above are basic to the subsequent execution of the plan and how widely accepted it will be.

Both military-bureaucratic and multiparty systems have engaged in this exercise before now, and therefore, there is opportunity for comparison. In what ways have the party and military-bureaucratic systems approached development planning? What are the relative merits of each planning process and what differences are observable? Are there differences in the results produced by the planning procedure of each? If there are, how significantly different are the results and to what extent can one theoretically associate such differences with the ruling capacity of each type of political system?

PLANNING AND DECISION MAKING: PARTY SYSTEM VERSUS MILITARY-BUREAUCRATIC SYSTEM

As discussed earlier, during the multiparty era the regions were much more individually powerful than the states currently are. This time-relative difference in power base is important in determining the dynamics of the relationship between the federal (central) government and regional or state government in the development process.

Between 1962 and 1966, the central planning institution, the National Economic Council, was not so much a unified planning institution as a congery of diverse, separate, and independent regional planning units all coming together to rubber stamp their individual plans. It was not that the central government had too little potential economic power to achieve better coordination; it was simply that party representatives in government lacked the will to achieve such coordination. At both the state and federal levels, "each minister energetically pushed his pet project forward, for official or private gains, regardless of the need for the maintenance of the plan's objectives and priorities."[2]

During that period, regional rivalry prohibited the establishment of some nationally desirable projects, and economic me-too-ism resulted in the duplication of plants and excess capacity in certain sectors of the economy, largely the industrial sector, particularly breweries, cement, and textiles.

The right of each government to pursue its own development policies was built into the establishment of the National Economic Council "since development was a concurrent subject."[3] The National Economic Council was given a clear mandate "to provide a framework of intergovernmental dialogue without encroaching upon the duties and responsibilities of the respective governments."[4] Thus, the development process lacked a coherent social policy objective and each regional unit went its own way. By 1962, this council still did not know how to achieve effective coordination, or how to give a sense of purpose and direction to development planning. As recently as August 1965, the council was frantically, but unsuccessfully, searching for an institutional formula that would enable leaders of opinion in government, universities, agriculture, commerce, and industry to consult on development problems in order to make an impact on public policy.[5] In tacit recognition of its own ineptitude, the council established a Joint Planning Committee to be its executive arm. Figure 5.1 diagrams the linkages of the various institutions involved in planning from 1962 to 1965.

Figure 5.1 shows that the federal and regional cabinets were equal and coordinate in their relationships to the National Economic Council and that the regional and federal development ministries were equal to the Joint Planning Committee. The Joint Planning Committee was responsible to the National Economic Council. The observable equality of regional and federal governments created problems of coordination and accountability in decision making for the National Economic Council. Since its decisions were not binding on any government (plans were changed without prior reference to it), it was not looked upon as an institution that could legitimize decisions. Thus, it progressively lost its credibility. Obayan characterized this council as a "body of compromises unable to give effective philosophy for the [1962-68] plan, and leadership to planners."[6]

Figure 5.1
Process of Economic Decision Making: 1962-65

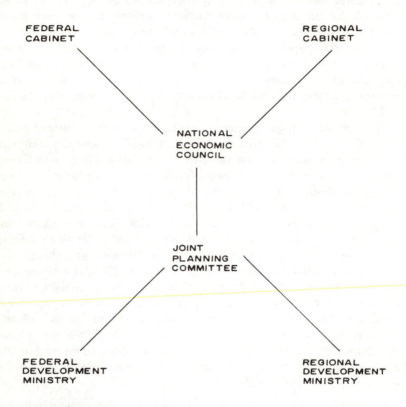

Another significant weakness of the planning process under the civilian party regime was the scope of participation, which was particularly narrow; the committee consisted essentially of administrative and technical officials from the government and a few counterparts from outside bodies such as the United Nations. Besides lack of participation by nonofficials (except for one or two intellectuals), the planning process excluded the private sector as well as the large rural sector. This low level of involvement contributed to the task of creating a nationally-coordinated advisory model without a broad social base for planning. Effects of this ineptitude were reflected in economic, political, and social consequences.

IMPACT OF PLANNING PROCESS ON ECONOMIC DEVELOPMENT AND POLITICAL STABILITY: PARTY SYSTEM

The intense competition and lack of coordination were reflected in the inability of the NEC to set definite national targets for industrial expansion. Within the iron and steel industry (a primary project for industrial expansion), it failed to give national direction in the choice of a site. This apparently simple problem of location, rather than other technical difficulties (such as lack of ore or fuel and subsequent transportation costs), held back the development of the project for more than 15 years.

First brought up as early as 1959, the NEC failed to reach an agreement until it was phased out in 1966. A technical group from the United Nations had recommended two alternative sites: one in the East (Enugu), and one in the North (Lokoja), with Onitsha in the Eastern region also a possibility. Each of the two regions directly involved initially wanted the advantage for itself and self-consciously prepared separate alternative reports to back up its claim. To complicate matters, iron ore was discovered in a third region (the West) and the NEC became completely helpless. Its proposed solution was the establishment of two separate mills (in 1964) and the possibility of a third one. This plan was inept and unworkable and further confirmed the body's ineffectiveness. The problem was not the bureaucratic institution's inability to coordinate activities (that is what they are most preeminently suited to do), but in its operation. The blame could thus be laid at the feet of the political framework within which it was working.

The processing of economic problems continuously rested with the institutional machinery of each regional government, a political process that progressively undermined the legitimacy of the federal government itself and led to its final collapse. It can also be inferred from this process that, since no additional institutions were created at the federal or regional levels, existing institutions were bound to collapse with increasing load.[7] Indeed, the final collapse of civil order and stability in the 1965-66 period was a culmination of the decline of institutional dimensions of the polity. Rather than arrest the progress of this decline, the political parties hastened the nation's collapse by deepening the highly competitive character of intergovernmental relations without enhancing inter-governmental communication.

While it is true that various Nigerian governments arrived at different compromises in different crises periods without going to war, during the party regime, the situation could not have continued much longer in the face of the almost complete undermining of political and economic institutions by December 1965. The National Economic Council (as well as other joint national bodies) failed to coordinate national activities in any sense, and it was aided and abetted by the national leadership to encourage regional parsimony.[8]

For precisely this reason, one cannot argue that the political parties would never have gone to war to solve regional/ethnic differences. The traditional institutional machinery for solving interregional conflicts had become delegitimated, and the federal government is said to have prepared the military to march on the Western state as early as January 1966.[9] There was a widespread belief that the Sardauna of Sokoto (leader of the Northern Peoples Congress and by far the most powerful politician in the country) and his southern ally, Chief Akintola, were about to stage a putsch of their own before the first military coup took place:

> The public is still largely unaware of the fact that a gigantic military operation over the Western Region was to swoop down on that territory on January 17. The incident that is associated with January 15 today was to take place somewhere later, that is, the following month. When therefore the significance of the state of emergency due to be proclaimed on January 17 was made known to us, it became inevitable that the operation of January 15 must necessarily take place before the dawn of January 17.[10]

Miner also stated that "there are some indications that (the Sardauna of Sokoto) was contemplating sterner measures to deal with the situation in the Western region."[11] Luckham concluded (in agreement with our position) that the existence of beliefs in such a plot helps to make a coherent, focused picture out of a confused and disturbing set of political phenomena, namely the *weakness of civilian institutions* and the rise in political conflict (emphasis ours).[12] Therefore, there is no mistaking the fact that economic and political institutions had completely degenerated and were incapable of further sustaining effective rule.

The federal military government not only altered the relationship between itself and the regions, it revamped the planning machinery. It scrapped the NEC and established the following structure as the framework for economic decision making.

1. Supreme Military Council. This organization harmonizes all national economic issues at the intergovernmental level. It represents the federal cabinet of the civilian era; it was not created solely to serve as the apex of the economic planning structure but carries on other functions as well. This council is composed of military governors of states and civilian federal commissioners.

2. Joint Planning Board. The board is composed of the permanent secretary of economic development and reconstruction (chairman); directors of the planning units of the federal, as well as state governments; representatives of the Nigerian Institute for Social and Economic Research; representatives

of the Central Bank of Nigeria; the permanent secretary of the federal Ministry of Finance; and the permanent secretaries of economic planning and reconstruction in the states. Its duties are to coordinate economic policies and development activities of the federal government and their agencies, and to examine all aspects of economic planning and make recommendations to state and federal governments. This board is serviced by a central planning office staffed with academic professional planners outside the general pool of administrators.

3. Economic Advisory Committee. This group is composed of senior officials of economic ministries, and representatives of universities and of the private sector throughout the country. It has the duty of advising the federal government on planning, economic, and fiscal matters, and of harmonizing activities of the private and public sectors.

4. The central planning office in the federal Ministry of Economic Development and Reconstruction.

Figure 5.2
Economic Decision-Making Structure under
Military-Bureaucratic System

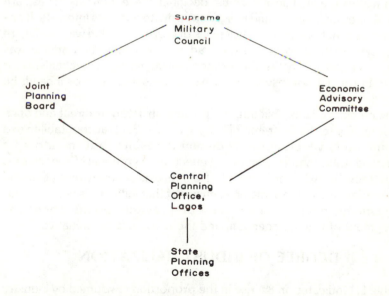

Figure 5.2 reveals the preeminent position of the federal government in planning at the national level. The state governments are represented at the Joint Planning Board and Economic Advisory Committee. The federal government indicated that the following broad principles should be

recognized for the planning exercise: (1) the concurrent power of state and federal governments in economic planning; (2) the need for an agreed framework of national objectives and development priorities; (3) the need to coordinate and harmonize activities between the public and private sectors; (4) the need to seek and take advice from appropriate quarters.[13]

While the JPE and the EAC have largely advisory powers, final decisions rest with the federal government at the national level and state governments at the state level. While becoming more preeminent at the national level, the JPE has given due recognition to state government initiatives at the state level.[14] This structure appears to be in line with the observation of Aboyade, who himself served on the defunct NEC, that now more than ever, centralization is necessary in the planning process.[15] The structure has also involved a greater number of diverse participants representing various viewpoints and interests. Its goal of harmonizing the private and public is far broader than the goal of the 1962-68 plan, which focused only on the public sector.

This structure also has its own problems. For example, there are apparently competing interests in the planning mechanism, and the body which makes the final decision must decipher these interests. These are political or ethnic, foreign and indigenous private business interests. It has been argued that one of the deficiencies of earlier planning was the failure of decision makers to seek expert advice, or when such advice was sought, to reject it. That is, the old mechanism provided mechanisms for advice, but it did not insure that it would be sought for, or indeed, be taken.[16]

One crucial variable built into the present structure is direct and open accountability to the Supreme Military Council. Such accountability to a national body which not only demands results, but monitors its achievement, has had an electrifying effect on operational efficiencies (as will be seen below). This method of emphasizing order, discipline and coordination, but at the same time, ensuring that initiative is permitted for the planning bodies, underlines our previous points about the employment of military coercion, and the allowance for initiative.

DEGREE OF INDUSTRIALIZATION

Table 5.1 indicates an 8% rise in the proportion consumed by industry and commerce between 1964-65 and 1971-72. The size of the percent rise does not reflect the actual amount consumed. For instance, electrical energy consumed by industry and commerce in 1971-72 was only slightly less than the combined total produced in 1962-63 and 1963-64. Significantly, only 36% is consumed by residential and other uses, reflecting a structural change in the economy.

Table 5.1

Electricity Generation, Showing Proportion Consumed
by Industry and Commerce

Period	Total generation million killowatt hours	Industrial and Commercial	% of Total
1962–63	755.9	394.7	52.2
1963–64	904.3	491.4	54.3
1964 65	1037.8	587.4	56.6
1965–66	1201.3	672.6	56.0
1970–71	1993.0	1314.2	60.0
1971–72	2096.0	1420.1	64.0

Sources: Central   Bank of   Nigeria.

The unusually high growth of the mining sector has resulted from the discovery of oil. It does not, therefore, reflect a general rise with respect to each type of mineral. However, the increased production of oil and other minerals reflects the more effective extractive capability of the present government. The Nigerian Petroleum Company has been established to prospect and mine for oil and, at the same time, to gradually take over the functions and assets of foreign-owned mining corporations.

Manufacturing increased more than 300% from 1963 to 1971. The slight decline in 1972 was due to the particularly high investment of 1971 and the effort to slow down relative to other sectors.

PROPORTION OF GROSS DOMESTIC
PRODUCT ORIGINATING IN INDUSTRY

Although there was a slight decline in 1971-72, Table 5.2 shows that the contribution of industry to the GDP is still substantially higher than for any comparable year before 1966. In the first half of 1973, manufacturing rose by 12.5%. While mining has been particularly buoyant, other divisions of the industrial sector have been performing relatively well too.

Table 5.2
Gross Domestic Product of Factor Cost at Constant
Prices (percentages)

Sector	1962-63	1963-64	1964-65	1970-71	1971-72
Agriculture Livestock, Forestry and Fishing	61.2	61.1	59.2	41	42
Industry Mining Manufacturing Construction Transportation	29.5	30.2	31.5	45	43
Others	--	--	8.8	14	15

Sources: Economic and Statistical   Review 1971
Central Planning Office,   Federal Ministry of
Economic Development and Reconstruction
Lagos, Nigeria   1971.
Second National   Development   Plann 1970-74
Federal Ministry   of   Information
Lagos, Nigeria   1970.

Table 5.3
Labor Force Engaged in Industry

	1962	1963	1964	1965...1970	1971	1972
Mining	44122	45773	48107	54000 53000	62173	71200
Manufacturing Construction	51283	52384	59000	61217 11435	127300	154000
Transportation (a)	30170	29252	30638	29586 32300	33184	34325
Total	125575	127409	137745	144803 199250	222657	260055

(a)   Railway   transportation   only
Figures   for   1973   are not   available.

Sources :   Nigerian Railway Corporation ,   Lagos, Nigeria
Annual Abstract   of Statistics,   Federal   Office
of Statistics,   Lagos, Nigeria,   1962-72
Economic Indicators,   Federal Office   of
Statistics,   Lagos   Nigeria   June 1972.

PROPORTION OF TOTAL MALE LABOR
FORCE ENGAGED IN INDUSTRY

Table 5.3 reflects the impressive increase in the total force engaged in industry. The 1972 figure is more than 200% of that of 1962. The rate of growth between 1970 and 1972 was about 26.7%, while between 1962 and 1965, the rate was about 13%. Not only has the labor force more than doubled in the two time periods indicated, but the rate of growth within each of the two periods is also significantly different. Moreover, there is a relative increase in the shift of the labor force to industry.

One of the declared aims of the federal military government is to reach full employment. The unemployment rate was estimated at 11.5% in 1971, a decline from 26% during the party regime. The government planned to create an additional 250,000 wage-labor jobs from 1970 to 1974. Efforts in this direction are reported in the first progress report issued in June 1972. At the same time, emphasis is placed on the expansion of the nonwage-labor sector, primarily agriculture and small scale manufacturing establishments. In contrast, the party system in the 1962-1966 plan period lacked a policy orientation and made no plans or projections for labor, and for the establishment of industries. This situation confirms the military orientation toward putting right what it felt the party system had done wrong, and where it felt it had not moved along fast enough. This is not to argue that the party system was inadequate, but that in the indicated period, it did not portray effective policy or plans for national development.

GROSS NATIONAL PRODUCT

Table 5.4 shows unusually high growth rates in the gross national product. Growth rate in 1972-73 is more than three times what was recorded in 1962-63. While these growth rates largely depend on oil, a report of the United Nations Economic Commission for Africa notes that these rates are also due to a recovery in agricultural output (which had been declining), and the general growth in the economy stemming from a wartime economy and the stimulus of a high level of development.[17] Table 5.5 reveals the composition of this growth. Improvement in agriculture

Table 5.4
Rise in Nigerian Gross National Product:
1962-65, 1970-72 (percentages)

	1962/63	1963/64	1964/65	1970/71	1971/72	1972/73
Actual	3.8	4.0	4.6	9.6	11	12.0
Projected in the Development Plan	n.a.	n.a.	n.a.	4.7	6.3	

Sources: (i) Africa Research Builletin – United Nations Economic Commission for Africa

(ii) First progress report, Nigerian National Development Plan, Lagos Nigeria, 1972.

Table 5.5
Sectoral Breakdown of Aggregate Growth Rate, 1971/72

Sector	Change in sector over 1970/71m	Contribution to overall growth %
Agriculture	40	2·0
Oil	93	4·7
Manufacturing	20	1·0
Building and Construction	14	0·7
Others	52	2·6
Total	219	11·0

Table 5.6
Sectoral Breakdown of Aggregate Growth Rate, 1972/73

Sector	Contribution to growth rate %
Agriculture	2·0
Oil	5·7
Manufacturing	1·2
Buildingaand Construction	0·7
Others	2·4
	12·0

Source : First progress report – Second National Development Plan.

contributes nearly one-half what oil contributes, while manufacturing has also been substantially important overall. Table 5.6 reveals changes that have taken place in a one-year period. Table 5.6 shows a rise in the contribution of oil and manufacturing. In fact, if oil's contribution were removed, residual annual growth rate would be 6.3%, which is quite impressive and equal to the project rate. It is only Brazil (another military regime) which, among developing nations, has recorded such high rates. It will be important then to examine the character of investment to determine how high development activities (other than oil) have been.

GROSS INVESTMENT RATE

Heavier investment than in prewar days has been recorded. For example in 1970-71, actual investment was £N381 million against a projection of £N355 million; in 1971-72, it was £N465.4 million against a projection of £N399 million. In both years, the actual amount invested in

Table 5.7
Structure of Investment in Assets (percentages)

Type of Asset	1964/65	1970/71	1971/72
Building and Construction	40	38	38.1
Industrial Machinery and Equipment	45	53	53.1
Land and Agricultural Development	15	8.0	8.2

Source :   First   Progress Report – Second National
Development Plan.   Lagos, Nigeria, 1972.

both private and public sectors exceeded projected rates. The progress report on the current plan indicated that if Nigeria continues to grow at the present rate, she would double her income by 1979. What are the sources of these capital investments? Revenue from oil has increased substantially from £N100 million in 1970 to £N300 million in 1972. Nigeria also had a trade surplus of £N247 million in 1972 — almost double the surplus of 1971/72. Domestic savings (private and public — through income savings, taxation, streamlining of the economy) in the 1970 to 1972 period were also reported to exceed plan projections. Actual internal gross capital formation in 1970/71 was £N762.6 million and £N930.8 million in 1971-72 as against the projections of £N710 million and £N798 million respectively. In 1962/63, capital formation was £N157.9 million, rose to £N172.7 million in 1963-64 and to £N196.1 million in 1964-65. The 1971-72 figure is more than 400% higher than that recorded in 1964-65 — the highest year before the civil war. This occurred only after the serious foreign exchange situation caused by the civil war had been fully corrected, and it can only be said to reflect creditable financial management by the present administration. The former federal commissioner for finance, Chief Awolowo, set a target date for balancing out and correcting the foreign exchange deficit, a target that was reached well in advance. Another source of investment is from foreign investors, who have been coming in increasingly larger numbers.

Although investment and the gross national product for the period from 1970 to 1972 have been considerably higher than the projections in the plan, the gross domestic product reflects an increase higher than the increase recorded for investment. The actual investment ratios in 1970/71 and 1971/72 are 14.4% and 14.7%, as compared with 18.4% and 18.9% projected in the plan. The ratios appear to be only slightly different from the 12.2% recorded in 1962, 12.6% in 1963, 13.4% in 1964, and are slightly under 15.18% recorded in 1965.[18] But when it is realized that the GDP has grown substantially between then and 1972, it will be seen that, in absolute terms, the amount of money invested has been very high. The first progress report claims that the association of lower investment ratios with higher rates implies a higher productivity of capital, or lower capital output ratio, than the plan assumed. A partial explanation of this situation is that, while the federal military government is investing as much as possible, it is also insisting on a fuller utilization of installed capacity which increases output with little investment. This supports our view emphasizing the process of accountability in decision-making structure and operational efficiency as embodied in the military organizational characteristics of order, discipline, and bureaucratic coordination.

Table 5.2 also reveals the changing structure of the economy, as reflected in the declining contribution of agriculture (from 55% in 1964/65 to 41.8% in 1971/72) to the GNP, while industry increased its share from 30% to 45% in the same period. Table 5.7 reveals that the structure of investment has been in a very large part responsible for this structural change.

At this point, it is important to note that the cost of defense and internal security has increased phenomenally over the prewar levels. The army now spends in two weeks what it used to spend in two years. Here Nordlinger's argument that the military assumes power for corporate interest assumes important dimensions. When it is borne in mind, however, that Nigeria has been engaged in a civil war, this position can be appreciated. The civil war found the federal army so ill-equipped that secessionist Biafra almost overran the nation in a few months. It is understandable, although not excusable, that large amounts are being spent to modernize the military. From the pronouncements of the military and their subsequent action, it is obvious that corporate interest was a minor secondary motive for seizing power. The question, of course, arises why it should still spend so much when the war is over. The answer can be found, in part, in the leading nationalist role that Nigeria has assumed in Africa, with respect to the still-remaining colonial territories and South Africa.

LEVEL OF INDUSTRIAL MODERNIZATION

This is measured by: (1) diversity and range of goods produced in the modern industrial sector; and (2) relative importance of domestically directed and financed modern power-driven industrial activities.

Diversity and Range of Goods Produced
In Modern Industrial Sector

The industrial policy of the present military government contrasts sharply with that of the previous civilian party system. The 1962-68 plan (drawn during the regime of the civilian political parties) had no specific policy guiding industrial development. It was content with administering various incentive policy measures to attract foreign and local investors. The only major industry it attempted to establish — the iron and steel industry — never got off the ground through the plan period. However, some important projects such as the Niger dam, the oil refinery, and paper and sugar mills were started. The present military government laid down the objective, among others, of ensuring a rapid expansion and diversification of the industrial sector of the economy. To this end, it adopted the following priorities for industrial growth. It wanted the establishment of: (1) agro-allied industries; (2) petrochemical and chemical industries; (3) greater integration, linkage, and diversification of the textiles industry; (4) an integrated iron and steel complex; (5) passenger motor-vehicle assembly and related industries; (6) expansion of existing industries for export; and (7) further import substitution in selected goods.

In execution of these policy objectives, the following industrial projects have either been fully operational, are being built, or have been established before the end of 1974: (1) milk and meat processing and packing; (2) palm kernel crushing plant; (3) fish trawling and distribution; (4) a chemical complex costing £N14.1 million (producing caustic soda, polyethylene, etc.); (5) other chemical projects include ammonia, urea, liquefied natural gas, super phosphate, salt refinery, and a second oil refinery plant; (6) an iron and steel plant for which a national Iron and Steel Board has been established.

To monitor these developments and make them operative, a national industrial development committee, consisting of private and public sector representatives, has been created. It is charged with the responsibility of setting up and operating federal industrial development centers located in different parts of the country. Each center is specialized in industrial raw materials in its zone, as well as in the zone's priorities in small-scale industries. Other functions of the centers are: (1) technical appraisal of applications for loans; (2) provision of industrial extension services; (3) training of entrepreneurs and staff; (4) applied research into industrial products, involving the design of products for small-scale industries and management training. Besides technical help, the federal military government is providing direct financial help by setting up the Nigerian Industrial Development Bank (to give loans to indigeneous entrepreneurs) and by urging all commercial banks to do the same. In response, several foreign banks, as well as locally-owned banks, have stepped up their advances and loans to indigenous entrepreneurs by an average of over 41%. All these are innovations, both in terms of the policy orientation and the substantive steps taken. They do represent a determined attempt to break through into self-sustained growth, which the party system was unable to pursue consistently.

Relative Importance of Domestically Directed and Financed Modern Power-Driven Industrial Activities

"Relative importance" will be measured by the proportion that industrial activities contribute to the total gross domestic product. Table 5.2 shows that, while the contribution of agriculture to the GDP has decreased by 20% between the two time periods indicated, that of industrial activities has risen by almost 15%, pointing out the increasing attention being paid to it and its output in the present military rule, as opposed to the time of the party system.

IMPROVEMENT IN AGRICULTURAL PRODUCTIVITY

One area where the present military government is associated with negative results is in agriculture. Production has been lower, in general, than was the case in the period from 1962 to 1965. Table 5.8 reveals the extent of the decline.

Table 5.8
Marketing Board Purchases of Principal Agricultural Commodities (in thousand tons)

Year	Benniseed	Cocoa	Cotton	Groundnuts	Palm kernel	Palm oil
1962/63	21.4	176.0	145.8	871.5	413.7	149.3
1963/64	20.0	216.0	129 3	786.9	401.3	147.9
1964/65	23.5	293.5	130.8	678.9	449.2	164.2
1970/71	n.a.	225.0	102.0	402.0	291.0	25.0
1971.72	n.a.	241.0	92.1	445.0	302.0	25.0

Source: Central Bank of Nigeria Economic and Financial Review, June 1971.

Table 5.8 reveals a decline in most crops in the two periods indicated. The decline was most severe for palm oil production, of which Nigeria used to be the world's major producer up to 1960. Cotton and palm oil continue to show systematic decline while cocoa, palm kernels, and groundnuts reflect an upward swing in production. These figures do not represent total actual production since they are only marketing-board purchases meant for export. Most of the palm oil is now consumed at home, while the increasing textile industry is buying up some locally-grown cotton. Indeed, the figures may represent, in part, evidence of increased industrialization. However, more data from Central Bank reports record actual decline. The Central Bank indicated that the monthly index of output of agricultural export commodities averaged 36.4 during the first half of 1972 (1960 = 100), the lowest in five years.[19]

However, several extraordinary factors have been responsible for this decline. (1) There has been unusual drought in West Africa in the last three years which has severly handicapped farming. (2) World prices of Nigeria's export commodities have declined by more than 15% in the last three years. (3) The poor prices paid to farmers by the marketing boards have encouraged both a shift to nonexport crops and to smuggling of export crops across national boundaries. (4) The general disruptions of the civil war have contributed.

While the volume of agricultural production is important, the really important issue is what is the effort the military government is making to redress the situation, and how does this compare with the policies of the previous party system. The military government took the following steps:

1.   It established the agricultural credit bank with the specific function of granting loans to farmers — an innovation over the practices of the party system, where no such policy was made. Such loans are made with the purpose of helping farmers purchase farm machinery (tractors, etc.), fertilizers, and seeds, but also to buy more farm acreage and expand productivity. The party system before 1966 established cooperative organizations for farmers. As a design to help farmers, it would have produced far-reaching results if pursued with a singleness of purpose. The problem was that these organizations became no more than political instruments, and any branch whose members did not vote for a party in government was starved of money. Again, it raises the fundamental issue of whether democratic political institutions (multiparty system) have established other institutions designed to enhance social, political, and economic development, or strengthened old institutions (chieftaincy, etc.) to perform the same function. The institution of chieftaincy was used perversely to entrench politicians in power, while the military-bureaucratic system is using it to govern and reach down to the grass roots.

2.   It reformed the marketing boards (as elaborated upon earlier) in the attempt to induce farmers to produce more and to combat smuggling. The rise in production of cocoa and groundnuts recorded in 1971-72 and 1972-73 are attributed to the direct effects of this policy measure. Movement in this direction would have been impossible in the party days, since the marketing boards constituted the greatest reservoir of money used for political as well as governmental purposes.

3. It embarked on the improvement of mechanization and optimum production with integrated processing industries. The present government organized an international trade fair with special emphasis on agricultural machinery and equipment in the last two years; it has expanded agricultural extension services to teach farmers the use of new machinery. What is particularly new is the effort to integrate production with processing at many local centers.

The policy measures described above reflect a greater degree of steadfastness of purpose than what the party system had, as revealed by the extent to which the policy execution is followed up and accountability strengthened by the military government. While agricultural production has shown a marked decline, it is clear that some precise, definitive steps are being systematically pursued to correct them.

RATE OF IMPROVEMENT IN HUMAN RESOURCES

Table 5.9 reveals the tremendous expansion that has taken place in secondary school and university enrollments. Secondary school enrollments jumped from 208,000 in 1965 by more than 100% to 425,000 in 1972/73, while university enrollments in 1972/73 were almost three times the figures recorded in 1965 (the last year of civilian party rule).

Table 5.9
Enrollment in Selected Nigerian Educational
Institutions (in thousands)

Year	1962	1963	1964	1965	1970/ 71	1971/ 72	1972/ 73
Secondary	195.5	211.9	205.7	208.7	-----	381.2	425*
University	n.a.	5.2	6.7	6.9	14.5	15.3	18.8

Sources: Second National Development Plan, Lagos 1970;
Annual Abstract of Statistics; Economic Commission
for Africa (671-752) August 1971.

In 1965, the ratio of pupils attending secondary school to the total number of that age group was slightly above that of 1971/72; the same ratio had risen to about 10% and the ultimate goal is 25% in six years. The federal government has, therefore, embarked on a massive secondary education expansion project.

IMPROVEMENT IN TAX SYSTEM

Ratio of Domestic Revenue to National Revenue

The military government's effort to improve the taxation system has been elaborately discussed above. The amount of revenue derived locally has increased, as reflected in the various fiscal policies of the government.

1. In the current plan, proportion of total amount expected from internally generated revenue is 57.9% of total, as against 20% in the development plan operated by the party system; that is, much less was generated from resources.
2. Because of increased internal revenue, the federal government has reduced the level of external borrowing from international monetary agencies, such as the World Bank.
3. It has abolished the 180-day waiting period on imported materials.

These measures reflect increased confidence in the ability to generate more internal resources. Private savings have increased in 1972 by more than 50% over the level recorded in 1965, while revenue from company and personal income taxes have increased by about 75% and 100%, respectively; oil revenue has increased by 400%.

Average Rate of Increase in Real Domestic Government Revenue

Table 5.10 reveals that between 1962 and 1965, rate of increase of domestic revenue was between 6% and 13% annually. But between 1970/71 and 1971/72, it jumped to 44%. This is unusual, since a large part of the rise could be accounted for by oil. But, as shown in Table 5.10, the growth rate would still be substantially higher, even if all the contribution from oil were removed, than it ever was in the 1962 to 1965 period. The rise

Table 5.10
Federal and Regional/State Revenue

	1962	1963	1964	1965	1970 / 71	1971 / 72	1972 / 73
Actual Figures in N's Million	148	154	169	192	377	531	638
Annual Per Cent Rate of Increase	___	6	9.8	13	___	44	21

Sources: (i) Economic and Financial Review – Central Bank of Nigeria, Lagos June 1971.

(ii) Recurrent Estimates of the government of the Federal Republic of Nigeria 1972-73 Lagos 1972.

of 21% in 1972/73 is an estimated figure, and indications are that it would be higher, although it is not expected to reach the 1971/72 figures. This suggests that the oil revenue might be reaching a plateau.

STRUCTURE OF TRADE

Is Nigeria still an exporter of raw products? Table 5.11 reveals that the export of selected crops, such as palm products and raw cotton, has declined. The decline in palm products might be due in part to lower production, but it is due significantly to the use of such crops for local processing. Palm oil, kernels, cotton, groundnuts, and rubber reveal the most dramatic declines. It is precisely in these areas that agro-allied processing industrial activities have been established. The upswing in the exportation of crude oil can be accounted for by the fact that Nigeria cannot consume the tremendous amount of oil products produced, and there is a flurry of international activity in this area.

Table 5.11
Nigerian Exports (N million)

Commodity	1962	1963	1964	1965	1970	1971	1972
Crude oil	16.7	20.2	32.1	68.1	254.9	475.9	541
Cocoa	33.3	32.4	40.1	42.7	67.0	71.5	53.4
Palm oil	8.9	9.4	10.8	13.4	1.0	1.7	0.2
Palm kernels	16.9	20.9	21.0	26.5	11.0	13.0	7.0
Groundnuts	32.4	36.6	34.3	37.8	22.0	12.1	8.0
Groundnut oil	6 1	6 5	8 1	10.0	12 0	6 3	5.0
Raw cotton	5 9	9 5	6 1	3 3	7 0	5 5	2 0
Rubber	11.3	11.8	12.1	11.0	9.0	6.2	4.0

Sources: Economic and Statistical   Review, Lagos 1971;
Central Bank of Nigeria   – Developments in the
Nigerian Economy.

However, comparing both periods indicated, it will be seen that there was a general rise in the exportation of crops during the multiparty time. Indeed, between 1962 and 1965, no general decrease was recorded for any crop except raw cotton, in 1965. While it will be reiterated that general decline in production accounts for low figures during the 1970 to 1973 period, Table 5.12, on imported materials, reveals the military government's greater orientation towards the establishment of industries.

Table 5.12 reveals that the average rate of importation of drinks and tobacco has reduced; since consumption has not been seen to reduce, it follows that local production has increased. This is confirmed by the fact that more tobacco and drink manufacturing plants have been established in all the regions of the federations. The decrease in the importation of mineral fuels and lubricants, coupled with the increased consumption, reflect expanded production of the oil refinery at Elesa-Eleme in the East Central state. Finally, the phenomenal increase in the importation of machinery and transport equipment (especially in the 1971 to 1973 period) can only point to one thing — increased use of mechanization either in manufacturing and agriculture, or in transportation. It is significant to note that the total amount spent in the three years, 1963 to 1965, is only just about equal to the amount spent in the single year 1972 on the importation of machinery and transport equipment. The only logical conclusion from this is that the military government has made greater progress than the party system did. The argument could be advanced that this increase might be due to the postwar reconstruction programs, but when it is realized that it is the policy of the federal government to approach reconstruction of war-damaged sectors systematically over the years (so it does not slow down further advancement of the economy), it would be appreciated that a substantial proportion of investment is diverted to the establishment of new industries.

Table 5.12
Nigerian Imports — Selected Products (N million)

	1962	1963	1964	1965	1970	1971	1972
Drinks and Tobacco	4.8	2.9	2.9	2·0	2·0	2.2	2·1
Mineral Fuels Lubricants	14·1	15·5	19·5	17.3	11·0	4·5	4·8
Machinery and Transport Equipment	48·3	50.6	74·9	92·4	141·3	215·0	210·2

Sources : Economic and Statistical Review, 1971. Developments in the Nigerian Economy, 1972.

In concluding this section, evidence has been marshalled to show:

1. that the change in degree of industrialization has been greater and more structurally important during the military regime than during the party regime;
2. that the rate of growth of the GDP during the military regime is twice as great as that recorded during the party regime;

3. that not only have heavier investments been made, but the direction of investments is such as to structurally alter the economy;

4. that industry has been modernized to a greater level than was the case during the multiparty regime;

5. that while agricultural production has declined during the military regime as opposed to the multiparty regime, far-reaching policies have been made by the military to correct the weakness;

6. that more determined efforts have been made to improve the level of human resources;

7. that improvement in the tax system has brought an increased domestic revenue as compared to the party regime;

8. that the structure of trade has been altered in such a way as to reduce the importation of agricultural products.

What is most significant is that the structure of economic decision making has been altered, and that the alteration is seen to be effective in producing the above results.

This evidence and data therefore support the basic hypothesis that, in Nigeria, the military has achieved greater and more rapid breakthroughs in economic development — as measured by the economic indices such as changes in the degree of industrialization, rate of growth of the gross national product, rate of investment, degree of improvement of agriculture, and changes in the effectiveness of the tax system — than did the multiparty system.

ORIENTATION TO INDUSTRIAL GROWTH

Building Heavy or Consumer-Oriented Industries

The Nigerian military government has given greater encouragement to the development of heavy industry, as opposed to consumer-oriented industry. Consumption industries are defined as those producing certain modern (especially western) gadgetry and wares, such as television sets, motor cars, and so forth. They are designated "consumption" because they reflect modernization without real development; that is, since there are no indigenous basic iron and steel and allied industries by which the machineries are produced, most of the materials are imported to satisfy the consumption tastes of the small westernized elite. Because the importation also reduces foreign exchange capabilities of a developing nation while it adds little to the growth of the economy, it is classified as harmful, in general, to the total economy. Importing the parts and assembling them in Nigeria may provide more employment opportunities, but it also serves to reinforce this consumption pattern. Evidence in support of this view will be marshalled by comparing the development priorities and pattern of investments of the military and party systems of government (but with particular emphasis on the military) in the industrial sector.

Priorities for Development: Industrial Sector

A report issued by the United Nations Economic Commission for Africa made this statement about Nigeria in 1969:

> As regards industrial policy, the Federal Government in effect contented itself with administering a number of incentive laws, granting income tax holidays and import duty relief on raw materials and a margin of tariff protection . . . *there were no clearly identified feasible projects, no set of priorities, no set of supporting policies and so very little government direction on the path of industrialization,* . . . after the attainment of independence . . . Except for the proposed iron and steel mill estimated at £30m, there were no specified industrial projects. The other specific commitment was to build industrial estates and provide for Development banks or Agencies. So it is difficult to measure achievement against definite Plan targets.[20]

The above comment underscores the emphasis already made concerning the lack of direction in economic development during the party era. It was important that, since 90% of the Nigerian labor force was engaged in peasant agriculture, and since 75% of the national revenue was derived from this source, the basis of the economy be broadened by diversifying it, in order to reduce the great dependence on the agriculture sector. A purposive development orientation would therefore be in the direction of establishing an industrial infrastructure, exemplified by the promotion of nonconsumer-oriented projects. Even though the oil refinery, cement, textiles, and a few others were started during civilian party rule, industrial projects, such as television set plants and housing estates, took precedence and were more dominant. The western Nigerian television project established in 1960 was proudly designated the first in Africa. Private indigenous investing focused almost exclusively on estate-building and construction, while private foreign investment concentrated chiefly on oil explorations. It became impossible, then, for the oil industry to expand into other industrial areas and be benefited by or benefit such segments. For instance, the establishment of petrochemical industry would have spillover effects into other industrial sectors, such as in the development of pesticides or fertilizers for agriculture. At the same time, the establishment of an iron and steel mill was a prime necessity for the building of other industrial plants, since these other plants would need the machinery.

What industrial priorities has the military set for the nation? To what extent do these priorities reflect an orientation towards heavy rather than consumer industry? The following order of priorities was explicitly set down in the current development plan: (1) agriculture-based industries; (2) petrochemical and chemical industries; (3) integration and diversification in the textile industry; (4) an integrated iron and steel mill; (5) passenger motor vehicle assembly and component industries.

Passenger motor vehicle assembly, the only consumer industry, is the last on the list of priorities, while iron and steel, chemical, textile, and agricultural projects are higher on the list. This reflects no less than a determination to expand the agricultural sector, while, at the same time, laying the foundation for a sustained industrial takeoff with the establishment of iron and steel mill and chemical industries. To what extent have these objectives been achieved? This question will be answered in two ways. First, we will consider what proportion of the above projects are completed or are ongoing; second, to what extent does the pattern of investment further reflect the objectives?

At the end of the war in January 1970, the military government established the Nigerian Iron and Steel Board, which was charged with the responsibilities of performing whatever preliminary functions were necessary and then going ahead with the establishment of the project. It was expected to be completed by 1974. The following projects were completed between 1970 and 1973:

1. agro-allied industries — meat packing, sugar manufacturing, drinks, and tobacco plants;
2. textiles — five new textile factories, manufacturing from fabrics to nylon pile carpets, were established in Ado Ekiti, Benin City, Ikeja, and Kano;
3. petrochemicals — pharmaceutical, fertilizer, and ammonia plants have been established;
4. automobile assembly — two plants are currently being completed;
5. others — pulp and paper, and footwear plants have also been established.

The military achievement in three years far surpassed the achievement recorded by the party system in industrial expansion in eight years. The above assertion is reinforced by the pattern of capital investment. Before independence in 1960, less than £N5 million per annum was invested in manufacturing industries, with foreign investment accounting for most of it. From 1955 to 1960, out of a total of £N91.3 million allocated for the public sector, only £N7 million was allocated for industry. Even though about £N30 million was spent on industries in 1964, only £N5 million came from the public sector. Since most private investment at the time was foreign, and since most foreign private investment went to oil exploration, other industries were virtually neglected. It is indeed to the credit of the present government that diversification and broadening of the base of industry were undertaken. Table 5.13 further reflects the pattern of investments by the military government.

Table 5.13
Projected Investments by Industrial Type:
1970-74 Plan

Type of Industry	Capital Investment in N's Million
Cement	3.00
Sugar	19.50
Palm kernel crushing	2.70
Pulp and paper	10.0
Combined fishing, trawling, e.t.c.	1024.0
Chemical	50.6
Iron and steel	120.0
Motor vehicle assembly	4.5

Source: Second National Development Plan 1970-74, Lagos Nigeria 1970.

The general trend in investment pattern is toward concentration in the area of intermediate and heavy industries, such as fishing and trawling, iron and steel, chemicals, and pulp and paper. Motor vehicle assembly takes a miniscule percentage of the total. Since many of these projects are ongoing, actual figures spent on them are not available at time of writing, although they are not expected to be far short of the projected figures. The only probable exception will be the combined fishing and trawling, which is expected to take much longer than the life of the plan to complete. The evidence adduced so far supports the hypothesis that the military has favored the heavier industry over consumer industry.

ECONOMIC NATIONALISM

The military government has moved in the direction of fostering greater economic independence, while cautiously preserving vital sources of foreign investment. This is opposed to the excessive dependence by the multiparty system on foreign investment. To what extent was the Nigerian government dependent on foreign investment during multiparty times? By what mechanisms has the military government altered this situation? How successful has it been? What have been the reactions of foreign investors and with what consequences?

Between 1962 and 1965, the Nigerian government was highly dependent on foreign sources for capital formation. In the 1962-68 plan (drawn up by the civilian party government), more than 50% of total investment was projected to be derived from foreign sources, as opposed to less than 20% planned for by the military government from the same source. This shows that the military has planned to alter the structure of capital formation by reducing the share of foreign capital in aggregate domestic. The question of how the military government will finance development will be dealt with below.

Other indices will be examined, such as (1) proportion of labor force employed in foreign trade sector; and (2) exports and imports as proportion of the gross domestic product.

In Nigeria, farmers expend over one-half their working time on the production of export (that is, foreign trade) crops. Since more than 80% of total labor force is engaged in agriculture, it can be asserted that 40% or more of the aggregate labor force is engaged in foreign-oriented export crops production. More than 30% of the farmers in the former Western region were fully engaged in the production of cocoa (a major export crop). Also, up to 1965, well over 70% of annual public revenue was derived from customs taxes — that is, taxes on foreign trade. It has been shown above that the alteration of the structure of taxation by the military government reduced revenues from foreign trade taxation to less than 60% in 1970-71, to 40% in 1971-72, and to about 33% in 1972-73. Since in 1962, and 1962 exports consisted mainly of unprocessed raw materials, it can be assumed that their production was geared to the vagaries of foreign consumption and trade. Since imports consisted of machinery and so forth, they can be considered along with exports as dimensions of dependence on foreign trade. Therefore, as in Table 5.13, Nigeria was more than 50% dependent on foreign sources for her gross domestic product. This represented a highly unstable condition, economically and politically. The evidence presented above confirms the assertion that the Nigerian civilian multiparty government was highly dependent on foreign sources for her capital formation, investment and trade.

The dependence of Nigerian government revenue, and in turn the nation's economy, on the foreign trade sector created an unstable, volatile situation. Since factors which are externally induced (world prices, demand curve and consumption pattern, trade agreements and diplomatic situations) are potentially destabilizing, this level of dependence will not only stultify the economy, but also hamper the pursuit of a planned growth. Besides, growing nationalism at home and the increasingly significant role of Nigeria in Pan-African politics dictate that Nigeria pursue a development pattern that reflects national independence, as opposed to dependence. The present military

Table 5.14
Exports and Imports as Proportion of Gross Domestic
Product, 1962-63 (percentages)

Year	Exports	Imports
1962	23·6	28·4
1963	25.5	27·4

Source :   Nigerian Trade Summary and Annual Abstracts of
Statistics.

government emphasized a policy that "on the social and political front, unhampered foreign ownership (of capital) will eventually lead to a situation where the economy is completely dominated by foreigners and it can no longer resist foreign pressures even in formulating domestic policy."[21] The government felt that, while foreign businessmen should be encouraged to invest in certain areas, other areas where domestic entrepreneurship was available should be reserved to Nigerians.

The Nigerian military government formulated the Indigenization and Nigerian Enterprises Promotion Policy.[22] By this, certain distributive trades and classes of enterprises are to be reserved for Nigerians. Schedule 1 of the decree lists enterprises exclusively reserved for Nigerians, while Schedule 2 lists those reserved for Nigerians, under certain conditions. Reserved exclusively for Nigerians are such items as advertising, baking, hairdressing, laundry and drycleaning, radio and television broadcasting, and tire retreading. These are not the areas traditionally favored by foreign investors and thus can hardly affect the inflow of foreign capital.

All enterprises specified in Schedule 2 of this Decree are hereby subject to the provisions of this Decree, barred to aliens, and accordingly, no alien shall, as from the appointed day, be the owner or part owner of any such enterprise —
(a) where —
   (i) the paid up share capital of the enterprise does not exceed £200,000, or
   (ii) the turnover of the enterprise does not exceed £500,000, whichever the Nigerian Enterprises Promotion Board considers to be appropriate and applicable in relation to such enterprise and
(b) If the paid up share capital exceeds £200,000 or the said turnover exceeds £500,000 (whichever is appropriate and applicable) where the equity participation of Nigerian citizens or associations in the enterprise is less than 40% and no alien enterprise shall be

established, on and after the date of commencement of this Decree, as respects any of the said enterprises, or continue to be operated otherwise as permitted by this Decree.[23]

The enterprises included on this list range from beer brewing, construction industries, manufacture of bicycles, matches, paints, soaps, and detergents; to shipping, and wholesale distribution. In its characteristically bureaucratic way, the military government appointed a Nigerian Enterprise Promotion Board to carry through the program. It has also appointed government supervisors (who are directly accountable to it) and whose duty it is to follow up the execution of the program and report back to the government. Again, the direct reporting channel and accountability can be seen as governmental coercive measures to ensure efficiency of operation.

In Section IV (b), the decree deals with large scale investment — that is, investment worth £N500,000 ($1,500,000) or more. The intention of the government in this area is to acquire participatory shares of between 35% and 50%, since most large scale industries are foreign-owned. The results have been that equity shares have been acquired at a high proportion from foreign investors in all sectors of the economy (banking, mining and oil, and manufacturing). In Februrary 1973, the military government acquired 48.3% of Barclay's Bank shares, 40% of the Standard Bank (both British owned), and 40% of the French-owned United Bank for Africa. Besides such acquisition, the policy is in force that all foreign banks operative in Nigeria must be incorporated as Nigerian-registered companies. All banks which have operated as branches of international banks with head offices outside Nigeria will operate as Nigerian companies. With respect to capital, the policy states that banks which are directly or indirectly controlled from abroad should provide a minimum paid-up capital of £N750,000 ($2,250,000). Penalties and corrective measures are provided against offending commercial banks. Relationship with the banks have been emphasized because they control all aspects of money and banking, both foreign and domestic. The situation deteriorated during the war so much that the federal commissioner for finance at the time felt that, unless there was a decisive federal government intervention in the banking field, the expatriate banks would continue to dominate the field.

The federal military government established the Nigerian mining corporation in October of 1972 to carry out governmental policy of active participation in all aspects of the mining industry. The government has also established the Nigerian national oil corporation, whose functions are not only to explore for oil with a view to eventually taking over from the foreign oil companies, but also to negotiate and hold shares from the foreign companies on its behalf. In pursuance of this objective, Nigeria has acquired a 35% equity shareholding in the Shell-BP Company — the largest crude oil producing company in the country (currently accounts for 66% of daily production). By negotiations concluded in June 1973, the agreements provide for a controlling share of 51% by 1982. Nigeria would pay for its shares in four yearly installments on the basis of the corresponding share of Shell-BP updated book value. The government has concluded similar negotiations with French-owned Safrap; it now owns 33 1/3% in the Italian-owned AGIP Oil Company, 51% in each of French-owned Occidental Petrol and Japanese-owned Teikotu oil companies. The federal government also owns 55% of all offshore concessions — an area that is already showing considerable promise. These systematic, but well calculated steps are not likely to produce sharp foreign reactions, which may be produced by outright nationalization or the immediate ownership of controlling shares in foreign oil companies. In the manufacturing sector, the federal government has also acquired between 35% and 50% of all new industries and is proceeding to buy shares in the old industries.

The reactions of foreign companies have not, in general, been hostile. For example, most big foreign firms affected have signified intention to cooperate.[24] The chairmen of the Standard and Barclay's Banks have welcomed publicly the acquisition of 40% of its equity shares by the federal government.[25] As a gesture of its good intentions, the Barclay's Bank has exceeded the lending quota to Nigerians, which was set down by the federal government. Nothing will stop oil companies from investing in oil production as long as they are allowed to do so. With rising gross national product and per capita income, Nigeria represents an attractive spot for investors.

There are powerful arguments which will lend acceptability to the indigenization policy. Indigenization, rather than outright nationalization, is internationally acceptable as a means of maximizing the flows of foreign capital to developing nations, with advantages to both sides. First, for the foreign investor, it is the only way of gaining a strong foothold in the local economy, since he will earn political acceptability and goodwill, both of which are crucial instruments in protecting him against the risk of instant nationalization without adequate compensation. Second, he will gain public relations advantages and local contact men. Third, he will be seen as identifying himself with the nation's development, since local talent has to be trained.

Nigeria has stoutly maintained that it has no intentions whatever of nationalizing any foreign industries. Successive commissioners of finance of economic development have publicly asserted that foreign enterprises are far from nationalization. The president of the Nigerian Association of Chambers of Commerce, Industries and Mines said that his association would in no way support nationalization of foreign business, but would favor full participation by Nigerians. The government has also stated that investors' contributions to development were "still welcome and appreciated."[26]

Besides such open public reassurances, the federal government still continues to operate incentive laws, such as tax holidays for new industries, special grants and incentives to war-damaged industries, and guarantees that profits can be repatriated. The repatriation of profits is organized on a time-delayed basis today, as opposed to immediate full repatriation in civilian party times. For example, part of a company's 1972 profit can be repatriated only in 1973. This insures that there will be reinvestment, as well as eventual transfer of profits. The present system of handling relationships with foreign firms appears to be more reassuring than has been the case in many other developing nations. The Nigerian approach forecloses the debate on nationalization and guarantees the expectation of the investor. While it cannot be guaranteed that the indigenization policy has had no adverse effects, foreign capital is still flowing in at prewar levels. Thus, it can be argued that the Nigerian military government has fostered greater economic independence while preserving sources of foreign investment, as opposed to the excessive dependence by the civilian multiparty system on foreign investment.

The crucial question that remains to be answered is how the money required to finance such a policy will be found. Nigeria has been forcing up the rate of domestic savings through taxation and budget surpluses. Also, the rate of personal savings has gone up. This has been confirmed by the experience of financing the war from internal resources, while simultaneously sustaining a reasonable level of economic activity. Also, the proportion of infrastructure investments will decline with successive plans, thereby making funds available for industry and agriculture.

Besides the tax and local savings, the foreign and local banks have been requested to grant loans to indigenous entrepreneurs. To this end, the federal government established in April 1973 the Nigerian Bank for Commerce and Industry, with the specific purpose of helping entrepreneurs who wish to buy foreign shares. It has found the money to do this from oil revenues, which are presently on the increase.

Other problems with the operation of the policy are in the paucity of trained manpower for management. Though the government has established training centers, the effect cannot be felt until sometime in the future. One important step will be to ensure the geographical mobility of the present trained manpower around the country.

In a way, the military government is substantively, but gradually, establishing Nigeria on the road to self-sufficiency in economic development. At the same time, it is legitimizing itself in power by expressing nationalist aspirations. National planning should be aimed at the transformation of the whole society, and must be directed at power centers of economic and political decisions. In the circumstances of Nigeria, a major segment of those centers, from the point of view of development possibilities, is still dominated by foreign interests. These interests cannot always be expected to coincide with those of the nation. The government has, therefore, resolved that in the formulation and implementation of the national plan, all its policies and actions should be guided solely by the best interests of the people of Nigeria. If Nigeria succeeds in making indigenous entrepreneurs buy foreign interests, is it not also succeeding in establishing a large and new cadre of private capitalists? To what extent is the military oriented towards socialist development, as expressed by movement towards a public rather than private economy.

THE MILITARY IN NIGERIA: PUBLIC OR PRIVATE ECONOMY

The military rhetoric has leaned in the direction of a public economy. The private sector of the economy, however, covers important developmental sectors in agriculture, mining, quarrying, manufacture, distribution, and transportation. The private sector contributes a substantial part of the gross domestic product, and about 95% of Nigerians are employed in private-sector activities in one form or another. Therefore, the private sector has always been a vitally important segment.

A structural shift towards public enterprise would require gigantic economic, social, and political transformation. The problem is made more complex by the indigenization policy, which requires the emergence of a new corps of private entrepreneurs, segments of which might resist such transformation.

The most direct way in which such a shift can take place is through an alteration of investment patterns, carefully gearing and channeling funds to the public sector. In the civilian party era, total private-sector gross capital formation increased as Table 5.15 reveals. Table 5.15 reveals that the rate of growth of the private sector rose from 8.7% in 1962-63 to 18.9% in 1964-65. The slowing down to 15.5% in 1965-66 might be accounted for by disruptions just starting in the nation. However, this is an impressive performance by the private sector, which is now moving away from agriculture to manufacturing and mining. Such structural changes might make it increasingly difficult for the desired transformation to take place.

In the 1970-74 development plan, the private sector is projected to contribute £N815.8 million pounds, to £N780 million by the public sector. Total national investment allowed for an amount of £N235 million. The federal government is expected to spend £40 million and the state governments another £N45 million. The ratio of private to public investment seems to be about 2.4:1 in favor of the private sector. Out of the £815.8 million to be financed by the private sector, petroleum oil investment accounts for £267.5 million. Since the planned oil investment is almost entirely foreign, while 95% of large-scale industrial investment is also foreign, it appears that even the plan allows for the dominance of the private sector in the major industrial fields (mining and large scale manufacturing).

Table 5.15
Total Private-Sector Gross Capital Formation
1962-1965

Year	In Million	% Rise
1962-63	104.1	
1963-64	113.2	8.7
1964-65	134.6	18.9
1965-66	156.9	15.5

Source: Nigeria National Development Plan 1970-74, Lagos, 1970, p. 225.

It is in the light of this apparent dominance that the indigenization policy and its method of financing assumes great importance. The indigenization policy requires that the foreign-owned companies be bought, or shares acquired in certain categories of them. There is extremely small indigenous capital to buy up the enterprises, so the federal government had to come to the aid of private sector. As the primary source of capital for the public sector, it has to give out large amounts of loans to the private sector through the central, commercial, and special banks set up for the purpose. Credit to the private sector has risen rapidly from £N239 million in December 1970 to £N295.6 million in 1971 — the bulk coming from the commercial banks. At the same time, credit to the public sector fell dramatically. This decline was a result of the shift in lending of the commercial banks away from the public to the private sector.

It appears that the balance of investment is in favor of the private sector. Besides, there are specific problems facing the development of public enterprises. Low level of skilled managerial manpower has hampered the development of public corporations. For example, all the six Federal Statutory Corporations, which were expected to generate a net investment of £N14.9 million between 1970 and 1972, are currently requesting the federal government for subsidy to balance their budgets.

A move towards a public economy, with its strong overtones of socialism, requires basic transformations in the economic institutions. It would require the discouragement of the continued growth of individual entrepreneurs — the opposite of which Nigeria presently has embarked upon. It could indeed be argued that the advantages of indigenization would be reaped by a few entrepreneurs. The present Nigerian situation actually confirms the opinion that the third-world military espouses socialist rhetoric while continuing to operate within a capitalist model.

The requirements of indigenization, the paucity of managerial skill and consequent poor performance of public projects, and the inability to change the structure of contemporary economic institutions have combined to lend no support for the hypothesis that the military has encouraged public over private enterprise.

The conclusion that can be drawn is that the military is fostering a mixed type of economy, probably much as the civilian party system was doing, especially towards the end of its regime. It could be argued that the problems of ruling a plural society such as Nigeria make the military sensitive to the consequences of alienating the business community — a substantial segment of the elite — at a period of instability. It could also be argued that there was no way of carrying the indigenization policy through without massive encouragement to the private sector.

NOTES

1. Nordlinger, E., "Soldiers in Mufti," *American Political Science Review* 64 (1970): 1131-48.
2. *West Africa,* January 1, 1973.
3. Aboyade, O., "Relations between Central and Local Institutions in the Development Process," in A. Rivkin, ed., *Nations by Design* (New York, 1968), p. 90.
4. *Nigerian Second Development Plan.* Ministry of Information, Lagos, Nigeria, 1962, p. 1.
5. Aboyade, "Central and Local Institutions," p. 92.
6. Obayan, E. O., "The Machinery of Planning in the Federal Republic of Nigeria," *Nigerian Journal of Economic and Social Studies* 5 (1962): 279.
7. Etzioni, A., *Political Unification — A Comparative Study of Leaders and Forces* (New York, 1965). Deutsch, K., "Communication Theory and Political Integration," in P. Jacob and J. Toscano, eds., *Integration of Political Communities* (Philadelphia, 1964), pp. 46-74. De Vrees, J. K., *Political Integration: the Formulation of a Theory and its Problems,* The Hague, 1972, p. 118.
8. Aboyade, "Central and Local Institutions."
9. Luckham, R., *The Nigerian Military: A Sociological Analysis of Authority and Revolt, 1960-67* (New York, 1971), p. 41.
10. Major Nzeogwo, Interview with Tai Solarin, Nigerian *Tribune,* Ibadan, July 2, 1967.
11. Miner, H., *The Nigerian Army, 1956-66* (London, 1971), p. 160.

12. Luckham, R., *The Nigerian Military*, p. 41.
13. *Second National Development Plan.*
14. *West Africa*, January 1, 1973.
15. Aboyade, O. "The Machinery of Planning," in A. Rivkin, ed., *Nations by Design*, (New York, 1968), p. 87.
16. Ibid.
17. United Nations Economic Commission for Africa Report. New York, February 1973.
18. Central Bank of Nigeria Report. Lagos, June 1972.
19. Ibid.
20. United Nations Economic Commission for Africa. New York, 1969.
21. Second National Development Plan. Lagos, 1970.
22. Decree No. 4. Lagos Ministry of Justice, February 1970.
23. Federal Government of Nigeria *Gazette*, April 1972.
24. *African Research Bulletin*, February 1973, p. 2322.
25. *West Africa*, February 26, 1973, p. 2907.
26. *African Research Bulletin*, February 25, 1973, p. 2494.

Chapter 6
Conclusions

What findings have been made and what policy implications do these have for the Nigerian government and Nigerian society? What theoretical and methodological implication does this study have; that is, what general sociological problems is this research a simple case of?

SUMMARY OF FINDINGS: POLICY IMPLICATIONS

By breaking Nigeria into twelve states from the existing four regions, and by fostering the development of integrating administrative and political institutions (which are serving as communication channels at the governmental and ethnic level), the federal military government made highly significant constitutional and political breakthroughs. By destroying the powerful but obscurantist separatism of the former autonomous regions created by the party regime, it has ensured that the possibility of a direct confrontation between groups is made more remote.[1] Since the states are weaker than the regions in terms of resources, and so forth which are mobilizable, they can now only come together in coalitions based on mutual interests. Since entering into coalition with others to attain a common goal involves loss of individual power,[2] powerful separatist tendencies are oriented toward more integrating channels. This situation has created opportunity for the development of cross-cutting interests and pressures (as, for example, in the movement of personnel and trade) among the several states. It will be noted that quite the opposite tendencies were observable during the party regime.

The policy problems associated with this development are many. Among the most significant is a possible ethnic separatism that may also develop based on the creation of states. The combination of ethnicity and the surge of enthusiasm deriving from membership is a new state must be subordinated to the larger, more consuming loyalty of the nation. The Youth Corps program as a service organization is a step in the right direction. The military government must encourage the development of new voluntary organizations with a nationwide appeal. Such organizations need not only be service-oriented, they may be professional organizations, such as teachers unions, medical associations, and so forth. Such organizations must exist beyond paperwork. Other specific associations that may be encouraged to be formed are such as the national transporters union and national farmers association. Even though there are national trade unions, their activities hardly exist beyond the nation's capital. The creation of states has extended the opportunity to expand membership of these unions. In the former regions, the drive for membership quickly reached a plateau, since each region had not more than one or two coordinating centers. With the division of the former Northern region into six states, the number of centers and, therefore, the opportunity to reach into the inner corners of the area is multiplied, probably as many times.

The military government also needs to create state bodies (like the old parliaments) composed largely of civilians, whose duty it is to ease the transition to the much advertised return to civilian rule. Membership into such bodies will be by nomination, under the criteria of service and fair areal representation. The military government has stated that one of its aims is to help build parties that reflect a national outlook rather than the ethnocentrism of the civilian party regime; unless such moves as suggested above are made now, it might be impossible to achieve the declared goal. Such bodies would also help to ease the load-processing tension on the administrative institutions described earlier.

The military government has reduced the income gap between the elite and the mass, and the development gap between the urban and rural areas more than the civilian party regime did. Even though the basis has been laid for a national incomes policy, special efforts need to be made to deliver ancillary services to the poor. Such special efforts consist of the intensification of the housing program for the lower income group and delivery of health services. Delivery of health programs can be improved through massive training of intermediate medical personnel and the introduction of community-based health programs which will utilize talent from the local community. Perhaps, in developing nations, the delivery of any specific programs cannot be seen apart from the general mobilization of society.

The distribution of power and the allocation of resources are fundamental to the continued existence of the federal system. While the preemption of an increasing number of policy areas enhanced effectiveness and the coordination of activities, it can undermine the foundation of the federal system by systematically rendering the states weaker. However, the states have been countering this development by coming together into coalitions and moving into areas into which the federal government might have wished to step. The states can be further encouraged to do this by continuously allocating more money to them, thereby making them less dependent on the federal government. This brings up the subject of the formula for the statutory allocation of federal revenue. Our opinion is that it is unwise to set down in detail any tight formula, as was done before the war. A better approach would be to set up general guidelines and operate the allocation system on an ad hoc basis from time to time. A permanent review body should be set up for that purpose. The logic behind this is that a flexible and resilient system will be operated by the discovery of oil, or the creation of new states will be handled without a radical change that could cause upheaval, especially during the life span of a development plan. The continued accommodation allowed would remove the topic from such a politically sensitive and volatile policy area, which it has been in the past.

The military has made a greater breakthrough in economic develop-ment, as measured by the enumerated economic indices. It has been shown to support the development of heavier industry rather than consumer-type industries. It has also achieved a greater economic nationalism than the party system, while avoiding outright nationalization. However, the military has not demonstrably preferred public-type economy over private economy.

The present economic prosperity in Nigeria, while due to military effort towards coordination and effective policies, is also due to the economic break produced by the oil boom. It cannot be overemphasized that, as a wasting asset, the revenue from oil must be harnessed toward the building of an economic infrastructure for a sustained takeoff into industrial growth. The military government's plan programs emphasize the building of roads (an important infrastructure) and the establishment of primary heavy industries, such as iron and steel. Economic development in the third world is not purposive without the development of infrastructures which, in turn, mean transportation and, particularly, heavy basal industrial development.

We recommend that far more effort should be devoted to manpower development, of which the nation is currently crucially short. In the Rivers state, the money was available, but the men were not. There was hardly any development statistic available in this new state — a fact which underlines the need for high mobility of available personnel. In the latter policy area, the military has moved more dynamically than the civilian party system. The snag, however, is that many of the personnel working in states other than those of their origin fear they might eventually lose tenure as locally qualified men become available. The federal government can allay fears in this area by encouraging legislation which makes a worker a citizen of a state in which he has worked for a specific and limited period of time.

Economic nationalism has had poignant political overtones in all third world countries for foreign investors. The recent move by Middle Eastern governments to nationalize foreign-owned oil has increased the fear in foreign investors. But the generally cautious approach of the Nigerian federal military government has been reassuring. Even though it can hardly be doubted that the ultimate criterion would be to own controlling shares, present steps generate mutual confidence in the future. It cannot be doubted that no nation worthy of its name would be happy to have its economy controlled by foreign concerns, with all the policy implications that may have.

Problems remain, however, in other areas. How will the government reduce the ensuing inequality which would derive from its overt encouragement of the entrepreneurial class in the bid to take over foreign interest? The effect of this move might not be apparent for another decade, although it is predictable that, unless attempts are made to redress the imbalance, further disruptions and instability might be expected.

The creation of states, and the development of new administrative and political institutions while strengthening old ones have enhanced the prospects for political integration and, therefore, for political stability. The fact that the civilian party system could not achieve the creation of states, but that it was only the military that could take such a vital step and successfully carry it through, sustain it, and nurture it, supports an important dimension of our thesis that it is only the military that is capable, at this time, of laying the basis of national integration and political stability in Nigeria. The precise mechanisms by which these have been achieved were elaborated upon. It is important to mention, however, that the collapse of political order and stable government created the social context in which the military became the only viable alternative source of authority in the nation. That fact alone is not, of course, sufficient to account for the success of the military.

Its organizational characteristics of order, discipline, hierarchy, and persuasion, on the one hand, and its determined purposiveness to restore order and stability, on the other hand, have been shown to be important factors accounting for its relative success.

Communal conflicts represent only one dimension of the cleavages causing instability in the body politic. Such a horizontal division is reinforced by vertical divisions at the class level, where there is a gap in the elite-mass income distribution, or the rural-urban differential develop-ment. All of these have been demonstrated to be potentially disruptive factors. The major cleavages must be considered in order to present a comprehensive approach to the problem. The fact that policies have been initiated, and seen to succeed in reducing the aforementioned gaps, reflect the extent to which the elite-mass and rural-urban gaps are perceived to be dimensions of the same problem. The efficient manner in which the private and public sectors of the economy are being integrated to reduce the income gap, industries are being dispersed, and other policies taken to even out development, reflects the directedness and the authority which military politics represents.

The division into states, the operation of effective income and rural-urban development policies, and the correction of other areas of weakness depend to a large extent on the distribution of power and allocation of resources — that is, the distribution of responsibilities and functions, and of the means to carry them out. This is a crucial problem area since, theoretically, the military, being a bureaucratic institution, preempts policy areas increasingly under its own jurisdiction to facilitate coordination of activities and policies. This process has facilitated the opportunity to build and foster integrative administrative institutions mentioned above. When a new policy area is preempted, state and federal coordinating centers are usually established. In the process of creating states, development-integrating institutions, there is a power shift between the federal (central) government and the states. With increased effectiveness in integration and administration of tax, and so forth, and with the oil boom, the federal military government has become financially stronger than the states in greater proportion than the federal civilian party system was stronger than the regions. At the same time, more resources are being allocated to the states by the federal military system than the civilian party government system allocated to the regions. That is, during the military regime, the political units (states) have had greater financial resources proportionately to carry out their responsibilities than the regions had during the party regime. The need to integrate and coordinate is related to the need to share power and allocate resources. The style of military politics analyzed in the body of this study supports the idea that the military preempts greater power to itself in the discharge of its duties.

In the empirical Nigerian case, with increasing economic prosperity revealed by the indices used, it is found that industrial unrest, and so forth, would not have abated if other means of control were not employed. It is at this point that the distinction between military and civilian-party political styles become more evident. For instance, in 1964, during the regime of the civilian multiparty system, industrial unrest completely paralyzed the country, and the government virtually became helpless. The multiparty government never actually regained control of the nation. It finally collapsed in January of 1966. Paradoxically, the civilian multiparty system used physical coercion by inviting the armed forces to help control the unrest at that time, while during the present military rule, the use of physical coercion to control industrial unrest has been at a minimum and is, in fact, reducing. Rather, the use of persuasion has been more prominent. The present military government has refused to interfere in the affairs of the trade unions (such as forcing them to unite or to settle internal quarrels), which would have been characteristically expected of a military labor commissioner. In other words, it could be argued that, since the civilian party system was incapable of handling unrest when demands were less highly politicized, it would have coped less adequately when demands became politicized. It is also argued that the military has become more able to cope by learning from its own failures and those of its predecessors. This point supports the main thesis that it is the military, at the present time, which is capable of maintaining political stability, as well as fostering economic development.

The present economic successes have been due, in part, to the oil boom, but also, in part, to the military style of politics, which emphasizes bureaucratic coordinating (order, discipline, hierarchy, and initative) at a time when the society is going through a period of unprecedented social differentiation. Evidences of this are the structural changes in economic decision making, which reflect better coordination in development planning, as well as improved accountability. It is, indeed, the bureaucratic coordination of activities, coupled with effective monitoring and accountability, which more adequately illustrates military coercion style in politics, rather than the sheer threat which its physical power engineers. That is, it is not the power of the guns which constitutes the elements of coercion I have dwelt upon in this study. It is more the operational efficiency, immediacy-directed action, and purposiveness illustrated by the organizational characteristics described above.

The Nigerian military government's movement toward economic nationalism as an attempt to control the national economy has the purpose of enhancing development. Besides, it has served to satisfy nationalist demands at home and has been instrumental in creating support from the business, intellectual, and political elites. In addition, consciously expressive ideological-nationalist sentiments employed by the military have been serving symbolic functions. It would have been impossibly hard to develop a nation's economy with heavy dependence on outside sources of help. Again, taking a broad comparative look at military regimes in Africa—for instance, Boumédienne in Algeria, Qaddafi in Libya, the military junta in Congo-Brazzaville, Mobutu in Zaire,

Acheampong in Ghana, and Gowon in Nigeria—the military style of politics tends to take on more nationalist overtones (at least in the countries mentioned) than civilian party systems in the same countries. Ghana's example is interesting since Nkrumah could be correctly described as an African nationalist leader, while the military junta led by General Ankrah has been described as antinationalist. This raises intriguing theoretical questions. Why was the Ankrah military junta so antinationalist while the Acheampong junta is so decidedly nationalist (and to some extent following Nkrumah's nationalist model)? This is certainly a fruitful area for research, but decidedly underscores one of the theoretical points made earlier: that an analysis of the dynamics of military coups is important in evaluating subsequent military performance.

Economic development, depending as it does on a solid industrial base, has been advanced further by the military than by the civilian party system. The theoretical underpinning here is that the military favors the establishment of heavy industry over consumer industry. While it has been demonstrated that this is so, it has also been shown that a road transportation system—a crucial industrial infrastructure with respect to economic distribution of raw materials and manufactured goods—is currently being given a bigger boost than was the case during the civilian party regime.

While the emerging picture is still not clear, it can be concluded that, in the effort to buy up foreign industry, the creation of a new entrepreneurial class is inevitable. This may have two consequences: the strengthening of the present nucleus of a middle class, or the increase in the relative deprivation gap, or both. It has been argued in theory that the emergence of a middle class, with its stable demands, its reservoir of resources, and its buying power and democratic outlook, augurs well for development and stability in the third world nations. While this argument cannot be discounted, perhaps it is also the middle class in developing nations that is most dependent for its means of satisfaction on foreign sources. It can be concluded that, unless internal resources are quickly mobilized and industrial takeoff quickly attained (by which manufactured goods are multiplied), the military may in the long run unwittingly be creating a class which will increase dependence on foreign economy, which the military has been fighting hard to avoid.

Secondly, what will be more readily apparent, in the short run, is a possible increase in the relative deprivation gap. Possible consequences are political agitations and unrest. This should not be exaggerated, since the government is, at the same time, encouraging the public sector. With increased governmental resources, the final picture is likely to be one of a well-mixed economy in which both the public and private-economy systems thrive together.

THEORETICAL IMPLICATIONS

The main thrust of this research has been to examine the extent to which the performance of the tasks of government and ruling has been related to the structure and organization of the military in Nigeria, comparing this at each point with the performance of the civilian party system of the previous era. Our emphasis has been on the uses of both coercion and consensus (coercion being a military organization value— described as order, discipline, hierarchy, accountability, and demand regulation, but tempered in modern times by the growing emphasis on initiative, persuasion, and compromise). Reliance on physical threat as the dominant mechanism of control having declined with the growing sophistication of the military in the arts of governance, the military organizational models seem more applicable to other types of collective effort to rule society.

The characteristics of order, discipline, and hierarchy represent elements in a bureaucratic mode of operation as presented by Weber. The military is a reservoir of these characteristics, and it has been observed that its activities are often guided by these values. The military has been characterized as "the armed bureaucracy."[3] With the collapse of order in Nigeria in 1966, and the increasing complexity and social differentiation deriving from modernization efforts, the need for coordination of activities become greater. Bureaucratic coordination has been described as a most effective way of handling the problems arising from increased differentiation and, therefore, the military became a viable alternative ruling group.[4]

The question arises: what special characteristics distinguish military-bureaucratic coordination from the civilian-party-system mode of co-ordination? The diacritical feature of military-bureaucratic coordination in Nigeria has been the force of authority, which derives from its insistence on order, the discipline, close scrutiny, supervision, and follow-up which produces strong accountability and thus effectiveness. The order and discipline deriving from a strictly accountable, bureaucratically coordinated organization system is the dimension of coercion stressed in this thesis. The strength and resilience of a military regime is predicated not upon its increasing dependence on physical threat to back up its commands, but upon an acceptance of its authority and legitimacy. What has been demonstrated in this study is that the Nigerian military, from the conclusion of the civil-war period to the present, has evoked its physical power less and less, but has acquired increasing legitimacy through economic development and by building institutions as instruments of government.

Perhaps the most critical factor associated with political instability in many African countries is the ethnic class and religious pluralism, as enunciated earlier in the Nigerian case. What theory needs is to begin reconsidering the role of coercion in the process of guaranteeing equity and industrializing these societies.

Coercion, as analyzed in this thesis, has permitted the Nigerian military not only to enforce norms, but also to perform a norm-setting function. The enforcement of norms and the creation of new norms are of great significance for the strengthening of the already-existing institutions of society, and for the creating of new ones where rapid social differentiation has created an unstable condition. In 1964 and 1965, the nonobservance of election rules by the civilian political system led to the complete collapse of the electoral system. In a nation just experimenting with the western democratic political system, strict observance of the rules of the game was called for. But because each of the political parties (with their bases of support among the separate ethnic groups) was more concerned with reaping rewards and establishing an expansive patronage system, the norms of election were not observed. Earlier, in 1963, ethnic obscurantism prevented the national census procedure from being legitimately accepted by the people. Indeed, it can be argued that what the people will accept as legitimate must be predicated upon an adherence to the norms which define the pattern of interaction between them and the government, as well as among groups within the society. The 1963 census, and the 1964 and 1965 elections were not accepted as legitimate by large sections of the population due to widespread corrupt practices. What is also of importance is that the people increasingly refused to accept other activities of government as legitimate; hence the widespread unpopularity of the Akintola government in Western Nigeria between 1963 and 1965. The declining legitimacy of one political institution rapidly spreads to other institutions of government and society.

A concomitant development of the decline of institutions was the spate of violent reactions and political disruptions, which were frequent and widespread from 1963 to 1965. The inability to arrest the progress of this decline was due not only to the breakdown of the electoral, legislative, and other political institutions, but also to the spillover effects of this decline into educational, economic, religious, and other institutions. For example, political and ethnic identifications were instrumental in the collapse of the higher institutions of learning in Nigeria, especially in 1965. Relationships among groups generated from hostility to enmity.[5] The consequent disintegration of the nation required a strong force that could reconstitute declining norms and establish new ones.

The military in Africa has often assumed power in an atmosphere of real and potential crises. This fact causes attention to be focussed on military performance. This element of high visibility, combined with the atmosphere of emergency that accompanies it, renders the need to succeed both crucial and urgent. When these factors are considered, along with the fact that new beginnings have to be made in building norms and institutions, the role of coercion in the form of systematically regulating demands, enforcing accountability, and demanding efficiency can best be understood and appreciated in the effort to reestablish the bases for democratic processes and legitimacy.

In altering the decision-making processes, the military cancelled out some of the old institutions, but established new and more centralized institutions with direct reporting channels to the supreme military council. The rigorous accountability demanded of all institutions represents a clear departure from the norms of nepotism and corruption that existed in the party days. The military governors have been observed to lead community projects, set examples with respect to the observance of duty hours, and generally demonstrate leadership qualities. It must be pointed out, however, that the military possesses its own weak points. The difference between the military and the party system is that corruption and other vices are of sporadic occurrence in the former, whereas they appeared to be institutionalized in the latter. The military has consistently punished offenders within its own ranks publicly.

The much agitated-for creation of states, and the establishment of guidelines for the dispersal of industries among the various states and for the sharing of resources and responsibilities, have been the bases for the building of new political institutions and, indeed, for a new society.

This norm-setting role of the military is different from merely making efforts to achieve a managed consensus around the goals of integration, such as Nordlinger and others have charged.[6] It is one of laying permanent foundations for articulating cleavage of mediating conflicting interests in Nigeria.

Since it implies norm-setting behavior, coercion becomes an indispensable prerequisite of any government. It is precisely the blind denial or the lack of concern with this dimension of ruling, especially in social science theorizing about the developing nations, which has been hampering the development of theory.[7] Levy recognized the role of the military as a modern institution in third world nations, but deemphasized the significance of coercion.[8]

Apter recognized the role of coercion by linking it with the notion of choice. Noting that the functional requisites of a government are the conditions necessary for the making of political choice, he argued that choice can be made only when there is information. Information creates the possibility of an alternative set of choices. It must be forthcoming to the government if the government is to function legitimately. If information is not forthcoming, there will be consequences. The presence of consequence is the distinguishing hallmark of choices. Without coercion, choices will have no consequences. Apter stated further that coercion does not necessarily require physical force, or even direct control. It may mean the laying down of particular values that define loyalty. It is a system of public discipline.[9] When the norms of accountability, discipline, and equity are being laid down by the military, a new system of loyalty is being defined.

Theoretically, norm-setting behavior is particularistic, to the extent that the norm-setting agency defines the new norms only in its own terms. That is, the new norms may reflect only military values and raise the question of whether the new values and the new loyalty can be maintained once the military returns to the barracks. What happens when the military is gone? This question has been answered in large part by demonstrating that military organizational values are, in general, converging with those of the rest of the society.[10] Also, the institutions being built in the Nigerian case study are those that will outlast the military.

Apter elaborated on his theoretical perspective by emphasizing the role of coercion in the allocation of resources in the developing nations.[11] This treatment emphasized the new trend which is taking greater account of the role of coercion. This Nigerian case study demonstrates that the overemphasis on consensus in the literature of the early 1960s is clearly shifting its focus to a concern with coercion as a means of industrialization and legitimacy. The extent to which this shift is decisive is debatable, since some recent writers appear to represent a resurgence of the consensus approach. Perhaps what can be concluded is that there is a bifurcation, and more case studies will influence the balance of the shift.

The view that the military is incapable of ruling ignores the fact that the military is quite capable of learning, or of adapting its internal organizational structure to the problem of governing a civilian polity; it also ignores the fact that the social forces and conditions in a society may require precisely the type of effort in military leadership of society described in this study. What has been demonstrated is that the military is both capable of learning the process of rule and of adapting its organizational characteristics to ruling. The hostility between civilian politicians and the civilian bureaucracy, in the era of civilian politics, compares poorly with the present cooperation between the military and the civilian bureaucracy. The negatively-oriented use of the chiefs and other traditional institutions by the civilian politicians in the past cannot match the effective use made of these traditional institutions by the military. Such views also ignore the motivation which guides military intervention. It has been clearly demonstrated that the present Nigerian military, both in its utterances and actions, has demonstrated a genuine intention to unite the country and set it on the road to economic prosperity. This does not mean that the military does not show signs of weakness (as, for instance, in excesses sometimes committed by some of its members). But it reveals that, in general, the military has performed as adequately, and even more effectively, than the civilian party system in uniting the country and developing the economy.

It can be concluded that the Nigerian military has proven capable of ruling a civilian polity as diverse in ethnicity, in language and religious beliefs, in the varying regional levels of development attained, and in class structure as Nigeria. One implication for theory, therefore, is that the military cannot be ignored as an important ruling agent in third world countries. Even if the civilian party system were to be reinstated soon, the situation that existed before 1966, whereby the military was alienated from society, cannot be repeated. It is eminently realistic that this be so to avoid completely alienating a section of the elite and thereby constituting them into a competing but alternative ruling group with proven viability. Were the military to be again excluded constitutionally from government, then it would be incumbent upon the society that the civilian system of government show itself adequate to rule. Janowitz argued that the military will intervene again, to the extent that it retains its organizational characteristics and solidarity.[12] It may be prevented from doing so if the domestic economic, civil, and political arrangements are effective. They were not so in 1965 Nigeria, and it is difficult to see how they could be effective in 1973, especially when the civilian party system had been out of practice for such a lengthy period of time.

What we have considered above raises the general problems of succession to the military government in Nigeria. What form of government would be most adequate? Should it be another multiparty system, a one-party system, a party system combined with a sprinkling of the military, or straight military rule? The size and diversity of Nigeria does not make it likely that a single party can establish its power at the center. While the creation of states has made this even more difficult, it lays down the condition that, in the event of a party system, these states must come together in coalitions to form parties. In the event that many new parties emerge based on statism, they have to come together into coalitions. This is why the administrative and political institutions analyzed are important in laying the bases for integration.

The prospects of a party system of government are fraught with dangers. Whereas in many industrialized democracies, differences based on party emerge only at election times or in times of crises, in Nigeria, the man carrying a particular party card is constantly aware of his own affiliation and those of his opponents. This is in part because of the political power and patronage (contracts, scholarships, offices, social facilities) which the party in government enjoys.[13]

On the other hand, the one-party system becomes so oligarchical (as in the case of Nkrumah's Convention People's Party) that it becomes separated from the people. In fact, many of the one-party systems were more distortions of the multiparty system. Our argument is not to stress that the democratic multiparty system cannot succeed in ruling, but that the task of building political and administrative instruments has not been as adequately performed by them as by the military in Nigeria.

While it has been demonstrated that the military is capable of ruling, the weaknesses of the military as a ruler must also be weighed against those of the party system enumerated above. The elements of coercion, deriving from the military form of bureaucratic coordination (order, discipline, etc.), and regulation of demands imply a particularization of interest, in terms of superimposing its own values on the society. Military bureaucratization of society may have important limitations. First, military organizational characteristics of order and discipline may behave like threshold variables. That is, they may act to raise the level of development (which was initially low) rapidly, but may soon reach a plateau, beyond which development slows down but may be sustained at that level. At such a point, the initial enthusiastic response to military rule may gradually turn sour and degenerate into hostility. It is being pointed out that the Nigerian economic boom is reaching a plateau.[14] Again, at such points the clamor to return to civilian party rule may rise. While this has not happened as yet in Nigeria, comments in the newspapers reveal that certain sections are getting a little restless.

It is also at such a point noted above that factionalism within the military becomes a critical factor since some factions may want to return to the barracks, while others want more rapid development to demonstrate to the general population their ability to rule. This point emphasizes the methodological point raised earlier that the internal dynamics of a military coup are important clues to its subsequent performance. Coups have occurred as a result of the cleavages within society and within the military organization itself. In the Nigerian case, there were cleavages within the society which were later carried into the military ranks.

Within the society, there were strains at the horizontal level (communal conflicts) and at the vertical level (elite-mass gap). These cleavages had echoes in the military, where both the January and July coups of 1966 had ethnic overtones. But what was important in both coups was the character of cohort cohesiveness of the officer corps (a vertical source of organizational cleavage). This vertical cohort cohesiveness is related to ethnic divisions in the society, since the January 1966 coup was organized and executed by a small 1959-61 clique of Sandhurst trained officers, all but one of whom came from the same ethnic group. Organizationally, strains within the military have often occurred among sets of cohorts. Where this coincides with strains in the society, as was the case in Nigeria in January 1966, the likelihood of military intervention is considerably increased.

The Nigerian civil war resulted in a foreshortening of the command hierarchy. Several officers were killed and a reshuffling of cohort membership occurred. Some members of the original cohort died, others were promoted, and others have remained in their old ranks. The decimation of the old cohorts removed the immediate fear that they would remain as a nodal focus of cleavage. But it could be argued that the expansion that occurred in the military organization had given rise to extensive new cohorts. Will they form new nodal points of cleavage within the military organization?

First, the creation of the states tended to deemphasize the old ethnic hegemony, especially as the old Northern region would no longer be perceived as the powerful threat it had always represented. That is, the creation of states will have some salutary effects on the military organization itself. The former fear and distrust is likely to be replaced by cooperation and greater trust among the officers. The theoretical notion that the military is a melting pot for ethnic pluralism and differences can better be realized once basic elements of distrust are removed.

The second factor is the personality and the background of the Nigerian head of state. A Christian (son of a church minister) from a minority ethnic group coming from a predominantly Muslim section of the country, Gowon has had tremendous appeal to the southern peoples (Ibos, Yorubas, Benins, Ijaws, Efiks, Itsekiris, etc.). The southern ethnic groups had always feared the size and hegemony of the north, and a leader emerging from the majority ethnic group in the north may not have been as acceptable as Gowon. Within the military organization, Gowon's credentials (high school diploma, Sandhurst and other staff training) represent a cross between noncommissioned officers who have been promoted and the younger university graduates who have been commissioned.

Probably far more important than these credentials are the reconciliatory and compromising steps which have been widely recognized as Gowon's leadership attributes. Since the end of the civil war, he has initiated such a reconstruction and reconciliation process[15] that many foreign journalists have wondered whether there was a civil war. He has emerged, therefore, as a central unifying figure, both within the military and in the Nigerian society at large. But whether there will be factionalism depends not only on these qualities, but also on the resilience of the military organization in resisting influence from the strains in the rest of the society.

Since military organizational characteristics, in the context of ruling, may behave in this threshold manner, it can be concluded that they are eminently suited for short periods, especially when civilian party systems break down. It is quite possible to have a civilian-military-civilian-military typology in developing nations. This is what has happened in Ghana in the space of six years, and in Sierra Leone and some other African, Asian, and Latin American countries. It may be that what Nigeria, as well as those other countries need, is to reconsider the general role of the military in development. That is, a system involving the civilian politicians, the military, and the civilian bureaucracy might work most adequately. The distribution of power must be such that social policy is not subordinated to party policy. What theory needs is to begin to reconsider the role of coercion in the process of guaranteeing equity in the developing nations. This study of Nigeria militarism is an effort to show, in a concrete setting, how coercion does not automatically imply dictatorship, but may serve the purposes of democratizing as well as industrializing a society.

NOTES

1. This assertion should be considered in the perspective of the recent provisional census figures, which again raises the sceptre of a northern domination of the south.
2. Coleman, James, "Loss of Power," *American Sociological Review,* January, 1973.
3. Feit, E., *The Armed Bureaucracy* (New York), 1973.
4. Bredemeier, Harry C., *Personality and Exchange Systems* (in press).
5. Whittacker, C., and Barbara Callaway, "Social Conflict in Nigeria" (mimeographed) Rutgers University.
6. Nordlinger, E., "Soldiers in Mufti," *American Political Science Review* 64 (1970): 1131-48.
7. Huntington, S.P., *Political Order in Changing Societies* (New Haven, 1968).
8. Levy, M., "Armed Force Organizations," in *Modernization and the Structure of Societies* (Princeton, 1966).
9. Apter, David, *The Politics of Modernization* (New Haven, 1971).
10. Janowitz, M., *The Military in the Political Development of New Nations* (Chicago, 1964).
11. Apter, David., *Choice and the Politics of Allocation* (New Haven, 1971).
12. Janowitz, Morris, *On Military Intervention* (Rotterdam, 1971).
13. *West Africa,* January 1972.
14. *West Africa,* July 1973.
15. Hershkovilts, Jean, "One Nigeria," *Foreign Affairs,* January, 1973, pp. 382-408. Akiwowo, Akinshola, "The Performance of the Nigerian Military Government from 1966 to 1970," in M. Janowitz, ed., *On Military Intervention* (Rotterdam, 1971).

Postscript

The manuscript for this book was submitted to press early in 1974 and covered materials and data up to the first few months of 1973. Since then, several events have occurred in Nigeria which need to be updated in the book. Chief among these events have been: (1) the decline of the legitimacy of the military government headed by General Gowon; (2) the subsequent military coup and formation of a new government headed by the late General Murtala Muhammed, and subsequently by General Obasanjo; and (3) the military uprising of February 1976. This postscript is an attempt to fit these events into the general scheme of the book.

Our theoretical framework centered on the role of the military as an organization and focused on the relationship between effectiveness and legitimacy. The legitimacy acquired by the Gowon government declined rapidly from about the middle of 1973. The exact point in time is debatable, but the reasons for the decline are fairly obvious. The regime began to depart significantly from the tenets, principles, and organizational characteristics of the military. First, General Gowon's authority over the state military governors declined appreciably, as evidenced by his inability to carry out his plan to move these governors around. (The present regime has moved several governors around, thus emphasizing, in no uncertain terms, where authority lies in the military setup.) Each military governor became a little "lord" over his territory, and the central defining authority which still remains pivotal to any effective military organization became visibly and progressively weaker. It has been argued in this book that the military will remain a force to be reckoned with in modernizing societies to the extent that it remains an effective organization. This argument was valid then as it is now. There can be no arguing the fact that the present regime came to power not only to correct anomalies in the body politic, but also to arrest the progress of the decline in military organizational characteristics and thereby restore the image of the military as an efficient, effective organization.

Evidence brought forward almost daily in the Nigerian newspapers points up the depth of corruption of several of the military governors and functionaries of Gowon's government. One of the ideal organizational values of the military is a sense of patriotism and puritanism. The inordinate grabbing of public property and funds by such military men represented significant departures from these military values. General Gowon himself openly gave protection to one of his governors by declaring him innocent of any wrongdoing (even without trial) of an allegation of corruption on which that governor was later convicted. The regime wallowed in the same corruption it vowed to eradicate.

General Gowon's government also failed to carry out other advertised reforms, such as the setting in motion of mechanisms for return to civilian rule, military reorganization, and so on. On top of these were the problems of port congestion, rising inflation, and rising unemployment. Failure becomes more hurtful to the extent that the failing party initially advertised his unachieved goals. Visibility increases the opprobrium that accompanies failure and enhances the appreciation that follows upon success. Decline in legitimacy followed the obvious perception by the masses of the rapidly growing ineffectiveness of its government. People became frustrated when it appeared that General Gowon did not eventually want to quit office. He openly declared that the time for return to civilian rule was indefinite.

It has been argued that military organizational values behave like threshold variables when adapted to civilian rule. It moves dynamically at first, may then taper off into a plateau, and later may decline. It becomes incumbent on the leadership of the military to watch out for signs of this behavior. Indeed, the visibility of the consequences of military behavior on the polity makes it imperative that the military keep an eye on its own performance. Since a measure of order was restored after the civil war, the search for stability became a second-order priority, behind a dynamic movement of the economy, the raising of awareness, and the mobilization of the masses for greater things to come. It was precisely in this area that General Gowon failed to display the dynamic leadership necessary to give a sense of direction and purpose to a society struggling to find new ideals. But it is also precisely in establishing a new awareness, creating a wider consciousness based on the relevant social issues of the day (census, port decongestion, creation of new states and capital, task forces on several pressing issues) that the present regime has captured the hearts of Nigerians.

The effort of this writer is not to compare two military regimes, as it was, in the main body of the book, to compare the military organization with the multiparty system. It should be emphasized that the military has not changed basically in structure and composition. In fact, the July 1975 military coup was a bloodless transition. The leadership has changed and so has, one may assert, the goals and spirit of the organization. The behavior and performance of this regime is consistent with our theoretical position that the military is prompt and effective. One need only take a look at the catalogue of actions taken in less than a year to support this theoretical position. Some of these are: the cancellation of the controversial census, which General Gowon could not cancel; the effort to decongest the ports (brought about by the massive importation of cement by the Gowon regime); the giant and bold effort to deal with corruption, inflation, overcrowding, and establishment of a new national capital; the creation of more states; the effort to generate new standards of efficiency starting with massive retirements, and so on. One cannot but agree again with Bienen that the aims of a military junta constitute the key to an understanding of its subsequent performance. Thus, the dispatch with which General Muhammed's government has moved in several areas is a testimony to the sincere aims of its leadership.

General Muhammed was, until his death, as self-effacing as General Gowon was in the early days of his (Gowon's) government. But General Muhammed focussed the attention of the nation on issues rather than on his own person. Towards the end of his rule, attention increasingly focussed on Gowon's personality. Now the masses are able to see beyond personalities and concentrate on matters that concern their daily lives. The masses were afraid and reluctant to loose this new consciousness, as demonstrated by its rejection of the idea of a change in government and the unprecedented grief over the death of General Muhammed. Again, for the first time, all the various subnational units in this country came together in a voice of unity to mourn his death. Never have Emirs, Obas, Obis, and the masses converged in such a soul searching for unity and the ideals of one man.

In military sociology, it is becoming increasingly recognized that cohorts are strong potential groups for carrying out military coups (Luckham, 1971). To estimate the likely onset and success of military coups, an analysis of cohorts within a military organization cannot be avoided, since a strong sense of solidarity is demanded of the planners. The military coup of July 1975 was successful, in part, because most of the leadership fought together during the civil war. Besides the fact that they probably trained together and have progressed in promotion together, they have developed a strong sense of what the military organization should be. They also believe that the purpose for which the civil war was fought should not be thrown overboard.

From evidence, we have also seen that a group of majors (who had met during army conversion exercises) were planning their own military coup. Part of the failure of the attempt could be attributed to several factors, among them lack of group cohesion, and lack of goals and aims for the coup. If the military coup had been successful, what plans did that group have and how solidary was it? It was appalling to read the Dimka evidence on the design, organization, and execution of the coup plan. It is more frightening to visualize the drifts Nigeria could have been thrown into had the coup succeeded. The tenor of this argument is that the coup attempt had no place in the progression of the Nigerian polity towards civilian rule and the enhancement of national progress.

As a norm-setting agency, the military is laying down certain values which are ideally characteristic of it as an organization. Such values are effectiveness, efficiency, puritanism, promptness, order, and so on. The success of the present military government will be historically evaluated by its ability to sustain the current momentum of the drive to institutionalize these values in the body politic and thereby create for the nation a new vision, a sense of dedicated purpose and direction.

Appendix 1
Nigeria — Military Personnel and Hardware

ARMY

Personnel: 70,000

Organization:

   3 infantry divisions

   3 reconnaissance regiments

   3 artillery regiments

Major Equipment Inventory:

   20 armored cars (AML-60/90)

   150 armored cars ("Saladin")

      scout cars ("Ferret")

      APCs ("Saracen")

      light artillery (25-pound gun, 76mm gun,

         105mm howitzer, 122mm gun/howiter)

Reserves:

   Over 100,000 battle-trained men

NAVY

Personnel: 1,800

Major Units:

   1 destroyer escort (DE)

   3 fast patrol boats (PT/PGM: P-6 type)

   6 submarine chasers (SC)

   1 landing craft (LCU)

   2 corvettes (to be delivered in 1972)

Reserves:

Possibly 2,500 having war service

Naval bases:

Lagos, Calabar

AIR FORCE

Personnel: 2,500

Organization:

1 light bomber squadron (11-28)

2 fighter-bomber ground attack squadrons
(MIG-17, MIG-15 UTI)

1 light ground attack squadron (L-29)

1 training group (P-149D)

1 transport group (C-47, Do-27)

1 helicopter squadron (Whirlwind and Alouette II)

Major Aircraft Types:

56 combat aircraft

20 MIG-17 fighter-bombers

20 MIG-15 UTI armed trainer/ground attack aircraft

10 L-29 armed trainer/ground attack aircraft

6 Il-28 light bombers

52 other aircraft

6 C-47 transports

6 F-27 Friendship transports

20 Do-27/28 utility aircraft

8 helicopters (Whirlwind and Alouette II)

12 trainers (P-149D)

Reserves: Over 4,000 with wartime service

Air Bases:

Lagos, Kaduna, Ikeja, Maiduguri, Kano

Source: Catalog of Military Powers, 1972.

Appendix 2
Nigeria — Patterns of Ethnic Distribution

Ethnic Units	Estimated Ethnic Population 1967	Estimated Ethnic Percentage
A. Hausa Fulani (plus dominated or assimilated peoples)	15,370,000	29%
1. Hausa		
a. Daurawa		
b. Gobir		
c. Kanawa		
d. Katsenawa		
e. Kebbawa		
f. Zamfara		
g. Zazzagawa		
h. Auyokawa		
2. Fulani, 3. Jaba,		
4. Kuturmi,		
5. Kagoro, 6. Janji,		
7. Ninzo, 8. Kwatawa,		
9. Kagoma, 10. Bugaje,		
11. Kambari,		
12. Dakarkari,		
13. Dukkawa, 14. Fakkawa,		
15. Zabarma, 16. Gungawa,		

17. Shangawa, 18. Lopawa,
19. Busawa, 20. Waja,
21. Bade, 22. Kudawa

B. Yoruba	10,800,200	20%

1. Ahori,
2. Egba-Awori,
3. Ekiti, 4. Eko,
5. Ijebu, 6. Ijesha,
7. Jekri, 8. Cyo,
9. Ife, 10. Bune,
11. Ondo, 12. Akoko

C. Ibo	9,180,000	17%

1. Abadja, 2. Abaja,
3. Abam, 4. Alensaw,
5. Aro, 6. Awhawfia,
7. Awhawzara, 8. Awtanza,
9. Edda, 10. Ekkpahia,
11. Etche, 12. Eziama,
13. Ezza, 14. Ihe,
15. Iji, 16. Ika,
17. Ikwerri, 18. Ikwo,
19. Ishielu, 20. Isu,
21. Isu-Ochi, 22. Ndokki,
23. Ngbo, 24. Ngwa,
25. Nkalu, 26. Nkanu,
27. Okoba (or Okogba),
28. Onitsha-Awka,
29. Oratta, 30. Oru,
31. Ubani, 32. Ututu

D. Tiv and Plateau Cluster	4,860,000	9%

1. Tiv, 2. Gwari (Gbardi),
3. Mumuye,
4. Higgi (Kipsiki),
5. Bura, 6. Chamba,
7. Kaje, 8. Jari,
9. Eggan, 10. Kobchi,
11. Angas, 12. Birom,
13. Yergan, 14. Pangu,
15. Koro, 16. Basa,
17. Bokoro, 18. Bankal,
19. Gwandara, 20. Mada,

21. Afunu, 22. Gade,
23. Bassa Komo,
24. Burmawa, 25. Ankwai,
26. Ron, 27. Mirriam,
28. Mama Plateau,
29. Rukuba, 30. Njai,
31. Gude, 32. Komma Vomni,
33. Ndorawa, 34. Glavuda,
35. Jubu, 36. Tigon,
37. Mara

E. Ibibio and Semi-Bantu type   3,240,000   6%
   1. Ibibio, 2. Anang,
   3. Ogoni, 4. Efik,
   5. Ejagham, 6. Boki,
   7. Ekoi, 8. Yako,
   9. Ekuri, 10. Akunakuna,
  11. Mbembe, 12. Ododop,
  13. Orri (Ukelle)

F. Kanuri and Kanuri-dominated
   peoples type   2,484,000   5%
   1. Kanuri, 2. Tera,
   3. Bolewa, 4. Karekare,
   5. Bede, 6. Manga,
   7. Mober, 8. Koyam,
   9. Ngizim, 10. Mandara

G. Edo Type   1,784,000   3.3%
   1. Edo (Bini), 2. Esa,
   3. Kukuruku, 4. Sobo,
   5. Urhobo, 6. Jsoko

H. Idoma-Igala-Igbirra type   1,404,000   2.6%
   1. Arago, 2. Afu,
   3. Akweya-Yachi,
   4. Egede, 5. Idoma,
   6. Igala, 7. Nkum,
   8. Nikim, 9. Etulo (Utor)

I. Ijaw   1,083,000   2%

J. Bororo (pastoral Fulani)   957,000   1.5%

K.   Nupe   682,000   1.2%

Sources: G. P. Murdock, *Africa* (New York: McGraw Hill, 1959). P. A. Talbot, *The People of Southern Nigeria,* vol. 3 (London: Oxford University Press, 1926). 1963 Official Nigerian Census for Lagos, Midwestern Region, Western, Eastern and Northern Regions.

Appendix 3

Countries Under Military Rule (As of September 1973)

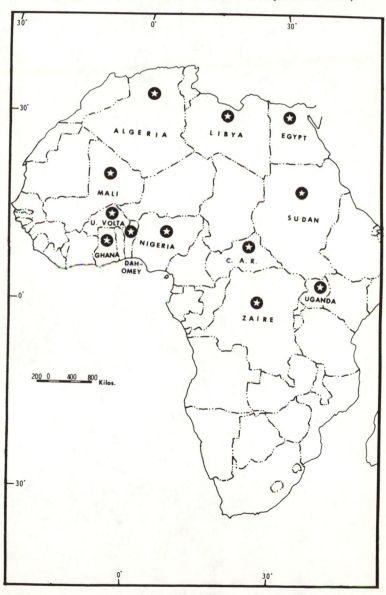

Appendix 4
Methodology

DEFINITIONS AND MEASUREMENT OF CONCEPT

We shall be primarily concerned in this appendix with defining and measuring two key variables, "political stability" and "economic development." Both are significant variables in determining national sovereignty, and the possibility and pattern of development in third world nations. However, economic development does not guarantee political stability, nor does political stability insure economic development. Political stability is a necessary but not a sufficient condition for economic development. There are many intervening variables (such as level of mobilization of the people, stage of development, effect of foreign influences), as well as strong interaction between the two. Studies that have used political stability and economic development as independent and dependent variables relied too greatly on aggregate cross-national statistical data, with the result that their conclusions are hardly applicable to specific nations.[1] This appendix focuses on the effect of military and civilian politics on political stability and economic development at two different levels: (1) where they behave autonomously (for instance, the relationship between the establishment of a youth corps as an instrument of political control and economic development can only be indirect); and (2) where they overlap (as in the political decision to site economic projects in specific locations).

Political Stability

Political stability is conceptually defined as the maintenance of political order and public order. *Public order* is defined as a stable situation in which the security of individuals or groups is not threatened and in which disputes are settled without resort to violence. *Political order* is the process of institution building, the creation of a stable pattern of political development (processes that include national integration).[2]

Public order is measured by a number of indicators. The first is turmoil which, in turn, includes the following:

1. riot events — incidents of political protest involving groups of people and marked by violence, as evidenced by the destruction of property, casualties, or the presence of police and riot-control equipment;
2. protest demonstrations — organized nonviolent gatherings to protest against a regime, cabinet, officer-politicians, policy, intended policy, lack of policy, previous action, intended action, or ideological position;
3. assassination events — the number of reported murders or attempted murders of national governmental leaders, governors of states or provinces, members of the cabinet, chairmen of city councils, and editors of newspapers;
4. reported governmental repression events — actions taken by the government to suppress or inhibit perceived threat to security of the regime or the state (these include reported acts of censorship and arrests made in connection with civil disorder).

A second indication is communal instability, which includes the number of armed-attack events or acts of violence committed by or involving highly-organized groups, large or small, with weapons of any kind, intended as protests or acts of revolt or rebellion against a regime, its members, or its policy; or an attack on groups within the society — religious, ethnic, racial, or special interest groups. Confrontations of the regular armed forces in a war zone are excluded.[3]

Political order, which is essentially a process of institution building, is very difficult to measure. The important thing is to focus on specific areas where political developments have or have not taken place. We have selected three such areas.

One area is constitutional and political development, such as the creation of states. The rationale for this selection is to evaluate, compare, and contrast the effects of development on: (1) communal integration, as measured by interstate flow of personnel, interstate development of common agencies (for development of other purposes), and the level of competitiveness among the states; (2) the strengthening of old institutions, particularly administrative institutions; (3) the development of instruments of political control (specifically the Youth Corps) which did not exist during the multiparty regime.

Another area is the growth of governmental institutions, which is measured by the degree of differentiation of governmental activities as follows: (1) governmental expenditure per capita, including the size of national government spending in relation to its population;

(2) government expenditure as a percentage of gross domestic product; (3) government employment per 1,000 population; (4) military manpower per 1,000 population; (5) defense expenditure as a percentage of governmental expenditure.

Economic Development

The term "economic development" is ambiguously and coterminously used to mean "economic growth," but very little has been written to clarify the distinction between them. Economic development must involve qualitative changes in the economic structure (say, industry, trade, agriculture, and investment). Economic growth implies, more than anything else, quantitative increases in economic indices, such as in the output of industrial or agricultural products. A net increase in cotton production in Nigeria may reflect a shift from cotton to the use of synthetic material rather than improvement in methods of cotton production. An increase in cotton production would be registered as growth, but if the increase came about as a result of changes, such as mechanization, which in turn influence the labor market, or from use of new cotton breeds, methods of planting, and so on, that would be development because it reflects structural (sometimes revolutionary) changes in agriculture and the economy. Most of the indices we will use are those that reflect structural changes. But in the case of indices which are controversial, such as the GNP, we will provide arguments for and against its use. Economic development shall be measured by the following indicators.

Changes in degree of industrialization. This is based on the average annual change in industrial output in constant prices, the change in the proportion of the gross domestic product originating in industry, and the change in the proportion of the total male labor force employed in industry.

Rate of growth of per capita GNP in constant prices. The GNP is an aggregate statistical index that reflects growth in many variables, such as industrial output, revenue, demographic changes, and so on. It has been widely used in economics to indicate development, although its value in concrete, real terms to the average citizen may not be clear. The measure is commonly used to evaluate the progress of nations (especially developing ones). Brazil's rate of growth of GNP has jumped from 4.6% per annum in 1964 to about 10% in 1971, while Nigeria's rate has moved up from 4% to about 12% in the same period. As an aggregate index, it often incorporates structural variables that may influence development. For instance, diversification of the Nigerian economy has been one of the factors responsible for the phenomenal rise of its GNP (although the crucial factor is its increased production of oil). Oil cannot be considered a factor in continued sustained development; it is valuable as a source of revenue to build industrial infrastructure. The criticisms against GNP as an index of real development are potent. Adelman and Morris contend that the tasks of socioeconomic political integration facing developing, fragmented societies frequently conflict with the goal of rapidly raising the GNP in the market sector.[4] For example, a lower GNP would be achieved if efforts were concentrated on integrating urban and rural areas, rather than on the urban sectors alone. Tacitly, these authors agree that GNP is valuable as an index, but they observe that efforts to develop rural areas will depress GNP.

Adelman and Morris asserted that most macroeconomic models focus on the rate of growth of per capita GNP.[5] Since our concern is with prospects for sustained economic growth, changes in per capita GNP may not provide a suitable focus, unless they reflect structural changes. GNP's inadequacy as a measure of movement toward capacity for self-sustained growth is strikingly evident from many cases of growth without development, such as Liberia. Baran claimed that expansion of the services sector would increase GNP, suggesting "economic growth," although in most countries it would be considered retrograde rather than a step toward economic progress.[6] A United Nations Economic Survey of Europe[7] noted that in the Eastern European economic communities, services not directly connected with the production and transportation of goods are not regarded as productive, and their value is thus excluded from national income. The report further argues that, for a poor country which is trying to develop its industry and reduce the underemployment common in service trades, the Marxist definition of national income has some obvious advantages over the more inclusive concept of GNP, which is suited to wealthy industrial economies. The Marxist definition is now more commonly adopted in the new nations of Africa, Asia, and Latin America.

As an index, the GNP appears to be a numbers game, in which composite elements vary from one type of economic system to the other. Yet economists have still not devised a more accurate, if less complex, index of national growth. Also, because it does include within it elements that suggest development, it cannot yet be discarded.

Level of modernization of industry. This is measured by the diversity and range of goods produced in the modern industrial sector. For instance, if iron and steel, cement, automobile, and footwear production are added to the traditional food industry, then quite a change is registered. It is also indicated by the relative importance of domestically directed and financed modern power-driven industrial activities. This index would reflect a number of other developmental variables (for instance, reduced dependence on foreign imports, improved manpower and skills and so on).

Degree of improvement in agricultural productivity. This is based on the adoption of such improvements as the more extensive use of mechanical power, chemical fertilizers, better crop rotation, and so on.

Rate of improvement in human resources. This is based specifically on the improvement in education. It includes changes in enrollment at the secondary level of education as a percentage of the age group, and enrollment at the university level as a percentage of the appropriate age group.

Gross investment rate. This represents the level of capital formation, with respect to the average ratio of gross investment to gross national product.

Improvement in effective tax systems. Improvements in the ability of the Nigerian federal government to increase its revenues over that of the states, relative to the prewar party government will be measured. (1) Change in the ratio of domestic revenue to the GNP. This will reflect the relative change in domestic capital generated for development and the effort to reduce dependence on foreign aid. (2) Average rate of increase in real domestic government revenue. The rate of increase will reflect the consistency with which domestic capital is generated. (3) Change in ratio of direct tax to total government revenue.

Structure of trade. This will be determined by the extent to which Nigeria has shifted from the exporting of primary products and raw materials to the exporting of processed and manufactured commodities, and the extent to which the exports have become diversified.

NOTES

1. For instance, see Nordlinger's "Soldiers in Mufti," *American Political Science Review* (1970): 1138-52, and other aggregate data studies of the world by Bruce Russett.
2. See Zolberg, A., *On Creating Political Order* (Chicago: Rand McNally, 1960).
3. Hudson, M., "Conditions of Political Violence and Instability: A Preliminary Test of Three Hypotheses," in *Sage Professional Papers in Comparative Politics* (Beverly Hills, 1970), pp. 243-93.
4. Adelman, I., and Morris, Cynthia, "An Econometric Model of Development," *American Economic Review,* 58: 1184-1218.

5. Ibid.
6. Baran, Paul, *The Political Economy of Growth* (New York: Monthly Review Press, 1957), p. 19.
7. United Nations Economic Survey of Europe, 1953.

Name Index